First Data Contamination Workshop (CONDA 2024)

Bangkok, Thailand
16 August 2024

ISBN: 979-8-3313-0161-3

Printed from e-media with permission by:

Curran Associates, Inc.
57 Morehouse Lane
Red Hook, NY 12571

Association for Computational Linguistics
209 N. Eighth Street
Stroudsburg, Pennsylvania 18360

Phone: 1-570-476-8006
Fax: 1-570-476-0860

acl@aclweb.org

Additional copies of this publication are available from:

Curran Associates, Inc.
57 Morehouse Lane
Red Hook, NY 12571 USA
Phone: 845-758-0400
Fax: 845-758-2633
Email: curran@proceedings.com
Web: www.proceedings.com

CONDA 2024

The First Data Contamination Workshop

Proceedings of the Workshop

August 16, 2024

The CONDA organizers gratefully acknowledge the support from the following sponsors.

Gold

Association for Computational Linguistics (ACL)
317 Sidney Baker St. S
Suite 400 - 134
Kerrville, TX 78028
USA
Tel: +1-855-225-1962
acl@aclweb.org

Introduction

Welcome to the Proceedings of the first iteration of the Workshop on Data Contamination (CONDA). The workshop is hosted at ACL 2024, in Thailand, on August 16, 2024.

Data contamination in NLP where evaluation data is inadvertently included in pre-training corpora, has become a concern in recent times. The growing scale of both models and data, coupled with unsupervised web crawling, has led to the inclusion of segments from evaluation benchmarks in the pre-training datasets of large language models (LLMs). The noisy nature of internet data makes it difficult to prevent this contamination from happening, or even detect when it has happened. Crucially, when evaluation data becomes part of pre-training data, it introduces biases and can artificially inflate the performance of LLMs on specific tasks or benchmarks. This poses a challenge for fair and unbiased evaluation of NLP models, as their performance may not accurately reflect their generalization capabilities.

We received 16 submissions, of which we accepted 13 for presentation at the workshop.

We extend heartfelt thanks to our program committee, our participants, and all authors who submitted papers for consideration—your engagement has been critical to the success of the workshop. We also thank Amazon, Google, and Hugging Face for generous sponsorship. Finally, we thank the ACL 2024 organizers for their hard work and support.

The CONDA Workshop Organizers,

Oscar Sainz, Iker García Ferrero, Eneko Agirre, Jon Ander Campos, Alon Jacovi, Yanai Elazar, Yoav Goldberg

Organizing Committee

Program Chairs

Oscar Sainz, HiTZ Center - Ixa, University of the Basque Country
Iker García Ferrero, HiTZ Center - Ixa, University of the Basque Country
Eneko Agirre, HiTZ Center - Ixa, University of the Basque Country
Jon Ander Campos, Cohere
Alon Jacovi, Bar-Ilan University
Yanai Elazar, Allen Institute for Artificial Intelligence, University of Washington
Yoav Goldberg, Bar-Ilan University, Allen Institute for Artificial Intelligence

Program Committee

Program Chairs

Eneko Agirre, University of the Basque Country (UPV/EHU)
Jon Ander Campos, Cohere
Yanai Elazar, Allen Institute for Artificial Intelligence and University of Washington
Iker García-Ferrero, University of the Basque Country (UPV/EHU)
Yoav Goldberg, Bar-Ilan University, Allen Institute for Artificial Intelligence and Bar Ilan University
Alon Jacovi, Google
Oscar Sainz, University of the Basque Country (UPV/EHU)

Reviewers

Rodrigo Agerri, Iñigo Alonso

Jeremy Barnes, Ander Barrena

Iker García-Ferrero, Shahriar Golchin, Itziar Gonzalez-Dios

EunJeong Hwang

Alon Jacovi

Yucheng LI, Oier Lopez De Lacalle

Ian Magnusson

Naiara Perez

Royi Rassin, Sahithya Ravi

Oscar Sainz, Hailey Schoelkopf, Preethi Seshadri

Yi Chern Tan, Kunvar Thaman, Kunvar Thaman

Keynote Talk
On the value of carefully measuring data

Margaret Mitchell
HuggingFace
2024-08-16 09:00:00 – Room: **TBA**

Abstract: Just as we evaluate models, we should measure data. Measuring data involves quantifying different aspects of its composition, such as counts of the top-represented domains, or correlations between sensitive identity terms and other concepts. In this talk, I will define the problem of measuring data and unpack how it can be applied to automatically curating distinct training and evaluation datasets for ML models.

Bio: Margaret Mitchell is a researcher focused on the ins and outs of machine learning and ethics-informed AI development in tech. She has published around 100 papers on natural language generation, assistive technology, computer vision, and AI ethics, and holds multiple patents in the areas of conversation generation and sentiment classification. She has recently received recognition as one of Time's Most Influential People of 2023. She currently works at Hugging Face as Chief Ethics Scientist, driving forward work in the ML development ecosystem, ML data governance, AI evaluation, and AI ethics. She previously worked at Google AI as a Staff Research Scientist, where she founded and co-led Google's Ethical AI group, focused on foundational AI ethics research and operationalizing AI ethics Google-internally. Before joining Google, she was a researcher at Microsoft Research, focused on computer vision-to-language generation; and was a postdoc at Johns Hopkins, focused on Bayesian modeling and information extraction. She holds a PhD in Computer Science from the University of Aberdeen and a Master's in computational linguistics from the University of Washington. While earning her degrees, she also worked from 2005-2012 on machine learning, neurological disorders, and assistive technology at Oregon Health and Science University. She has spearheaded a number of workshops and initiatives at the intersections of diversity, inclusion, computer science, and ethics. Her work has received awards from Secretary of Defense Ash Carter and the American Foundation for the Blind, and has been implemented by multiple technology companies. She likes gardening, dogs, and cats.

Keynote Talk

Evaluation data contamination: how much is there, and how much does it actually matter?

Dieuwke Hupkes
Meta

2024-08-16 09:45:00 – Room: **TBA**

Abstract: With many of the current "SOTA" LLMs being closed sourced and their training data inaccessible, more and more questions arise that relate to potential contamination of the evaluation datasets used to claim their results. Various claims can be found online that range from suspicions of outright training on evaluation data to inflate results to suggestions that the definitions of contamination used may be inadequate and underestimate its impact. However, even with access to the training corpus, contamination and its impact is far from trivial to assess. In this talk, I discuss common ways of measuring contamination and provide empirical data into how much they impact results for a range of LLMs.

Bio: Dieuwke Hupkes is a research scientist at Meta. Among other things, she works on better understanding how (large) language models generalise, what they (don't) understand and what that even means, and more generally on how they can reasonably be evaluated. She is excited about the new opportunities such models bring us and the new scientific challenges that go hand in hand with that.

Keynote Talk

Contamination in Web-Scale Datasets and its Impact on Large Model Evaluations

Jesse Dodge
Allen Institute for AI
2024-08-16 11:00:00 – Room: **TBA**

Abstract: We are at a pivotal moment in the history of AI. The AI research community has driven progress for decades, but over the past couple years industry has started to make significant advances in model capabilities while purposely being closed about how. In this talk I'll start by discussing different types of contamination and how they appear in the wild. I'll then discuss some of our work on building massive datasets by scraping the web, including Dolma and C4. I'll discuss What's In My Big Data, a toolkit for documenting the contents of web-scale datasets, and some of our results on measuring contamination in different ways across a variety of popular pretraining corpora. I'll conclude by discussing evaluation of large models, and how current evaluations have low construct validity and how we don't have strong evaluations for the actual use cases that users care about.

Bio: Jesse Dodge is a Senior Research Scientist at the Allen Institute for AI, on the AllenNLP team, working on natural language processing and machine learning. He is interested in the science of AI and AI for science, and he works on reproducibility and efficiency in AI research. He is involved in many parts of OLMo, a project to create fully open large language models, including creation of Dolma (a web-scale training dataset), Palmoa (an evaluation benchmark for language models), and incorporating ethical principles at every stage of the machine learning pipeline. His research has highlighted the growing computational cost of AI systems, including the environmental impact of AI and inequality in the research community. He has worked extensively on improving transparency in AI research, including open sourcing and documenting datasets, data governance, and measuring bias in data. He has also worked on developing efficient methods, including model compression and improving efficiency of training large language models. His PhD is from the Language Technologies Institute in the School of Computer Science at Carnegie Mellon University. He created the NLP Reproducibility Checklist, which has been used by five main NLP conferences, including EMNLP, NAACL, and ACL, totaling more than 10,000 submissions, he helped create the Responsible NLP Checklist which is used for submissions to ARR (replacing the Reproducibility Checklist), and was an organizer for the ML Reproducibility Challenge 2020-2022. His research has won awards including a Best Student Paper at NAACL 2015 and a ten-year Test of Time award at ACL 2022, and is regularly covered by the press, including by outlets like The New York Times, Nature, MIT Tech Review, Wired, and others.

Keynote Talk
A Sanity Check on Emergent Properties

Anna Rogers
IT University of Copenhagen
2024-08-16 17:00:00 – Room: **TBA**

Abstract: One of the frequent points in the mainstream narrative about large language models is that they have "emergent properties", but there is a lot of disagreement about what that even means. If they are understood as a kind of generalization beyond training data - as something that a model does without being explicitly trained for it - I argue that we have not in fact established the existence of any such properties, and at the moment we do not even have the methodology for doing so.

Bio: Anna Rogers is tenured associate professor at the Computer Science department at IT University of Copenhagen. She holds a PhD in computational linguistics from the University of Tokyo, followed by postdocs in machine learning for NLP (University of Massachusetts) and social data science (University of Copenhagen). Her research focuses on interpretability, robustness, and sociotechnical aspects of large language models.

Table of Contents

Program

Friday, August 16, 2024

08:55 - 09:00 *Opening Remarks*

09:00 - 09:45 *On the value of carefully measuring data.*

09:45 - 10:30 *Evaluation data contamination:how much is there, and how much does it actually matter?*

10:30 - 11:00 *Break*

11:00 - 11:45 *Contamination in Web-Scale Datasets and its Impact on Large Model Evaluations*

11:45 - 12:00 *Best paper presentation*

12:00 - 13:30 *Lunch Break*

13:30 - 15:30 *Poster Session*

Evaluating Chinese Large Language Models on Discipline Knowledge Acquisition via Memorization and Robustness Assessment
Chuang Liu, Renren Jin, Mark Steedman and Deyi Xiong

Confounders in Instance Variation for the Analysis of Data Contamination
Behzad Mehrbakhsh, Dario Garigliotti, Fernando Martínez-Plumed and Jose Hernandez-Orallo

A Taxonomy for Data Contamination in Large Language Models
Medha Palavalli, Amanda Bertsch and Matthew R. Gormley

15:30 - 16:00 *Break*

16:00 - 16:45 *A Sanity Check on Emergent Properties*

17:00 - 17:15 *Closing Remarks*

Evaluating Chinese Large Language Models on Discipline Knowledge Acquisition via Assessing Memorization and Robustness

Chuang Liu[1], **Renren Jin**[1], **Mark Steedman**[2], **Deyi Xiong**[1‡]
[1] College of Intelligence and Computing, Tianjin University, Tianjin, China
[2] School of Informatics, University of Edinburgh
{liuc_09,rrjin,dyxiong}@tju.edu.cn
steedman@inf.ed.ac.uk

Abstract

Chinese large language models (LLMs) demonstrate impressive performance on NLP tasks, particularly on discipline knowledge benchmarks, where certain Chinese LLMs are very competitive to GPT-4. Previous research has viewed these advancements as potential outcomes of data contamination or leakage, prompting efforts to create new detection methods and address evaluation issues in LLM benchmarks. However, there has been a lack of comprehensive assessment of the evolution of Chinese LLMs. To bridge this gap, this paper offers a thorough investigation of Chinese LLMs on discipline knowledge evaluation, delving into the advancements of various LLMs, including a group of related models and others. Specifically, we have conducted six assessments ranging from knowledge memorization to comprehension for robustness, encompassing tasks like predicting incomplete questions and options, identifying behaviors by the contaminational fine-tuning, and answering rephrased questions. Experimental findings indicate a positive correlation between the release time of LLMs and their memorization capabilities, but they struggle with variations in original question-options pairs. Additionally, our findings suggest that question descriptions have a more significant impact on the performance of LLMs.

1 Introduction

Large language models (Zhao et al., 2023) have demonstrated remarkable capabilities through alignment technologies (Shen et al., 2023a) such as supervised fine-tuning (SFT) (Zhang et al., 2024) and reinforcement learning from human feedback (RLHF) (Kaufmann et al., 2024). While the primary language domain of LLMs is English, the emergence of Chinese LLMs (Du et al., 2022; Zeng et al., 2023a; Bai et al., 2023; Team, 2023; Yang et al., 2023a) is creating another large community. A key question arises on how to effectively evaluate these advanced Chinese LLMs. Although there are various datasets for benchmarking Chinese LLMs, covering areas such as instruction-following (Jing et al., 2023), bias detection (Huang and Xiong, 2024), and code generation (Fu et al., 2023), the widely accepted approach involves gathering multiple-choice questions from human exams to serve as a benchmark for assessing Chinese LLMs across a range of subjects, thereby establishing a standardized testing framework for Chinese LLMs.

Several Chinese LLMs have made significant progress on discipline knowledge benchmarks (Huang et al., 2023; Liu et al., 2023a; Li et al., 2023; Gu et al., 2024). Current results obtained in these benchmarks indicate that the performance of certain Chinese LLMs is approaching that of GPT-4 (OpenAI, 2023). However, these benchmarks currently rely solely on accuracy as the primary evaluation metric, offering limited insights into assessment results. Moreover, discipline knowledge benchmarks usually collect questions from publicly available online sources, which could potentially overlap with LLM pre-training data. Additionally, once benchmarks are released, developers might unconsciously use them as training data for their LLMs. This introduces challenges related to data contamination and leakage, leading to misleading progress assessments.

Existing efforts aim to detect data contamination through various methods (Shi et al., 2024b; Oren et al., 2023; Yang et al., 2023b). For instance, Shi et al. (2024b) introduce a technique for identifying data contamination without relying on references. However, it has been observed by Yang et al. (2023b) that existing methods struggle to detect altered questions, prompting them to utilize LLMs for question rewriting to enhance detection capabilities. Despite these advancements, a com-

‡Corresponding author.

Proceedings of the 1st Workshop on Data Contamination (CONDA), pages 1–12
August 16, 2024

prehensive analysis for Chinese LLMs on this issue is still lacking.

In this paper, we conduct a thorough investigation into the advancements of Chinese LLMs in the field of discipline knowledge based on the M3KE benchmark (Liu et al., 2023a). Our analysis spans two key dimensions: memorization and robustness. These dimensions offer a multi-faceted approach to evaluating Chinese LLMs beyond mere accuracy.

For the memorization dimension, we have employed three sub-dimensions to assess the models. Initially, we evaluate the ability of Chinese LLMs to memorize questions and options from the M3KE dataset under various conditions like zero-shot and few-shot scenarios. Subsequently, we fine-tune an LLM on M3KE using different proportions to compare genuine contamination with instances where contamination is unclear. Lastly, we evaluate six LLMs by removing the questions and considering only the options as input based on a hypothesis that LLMs are likely to predict correct option without the question if they have memorized those test data.

In the robustness dimension, we also have utilized three sub-methods, including shuffling option orders, question rewriting by GPT-4 (OpenAI, 2023), and a combination of rewritten questions and shuffled options. This approach allows for a comprehensive comparison among Chinese LLMs whether those LLMs response to changes in sample description from the benchmark.

Our study involves two sets of Chinese LLMs for a more thorough investigation. The first group comprises ChatGLM models, such as ChatGLM1-6B,[1] ChatGLM2-6B,[2] and ChatGLM3-6B,[3] which are based on the same pre-trained LLM (Du et al., 2022; Zeng et al., 2023a) of identical size but varying versions. The second group consists of LLMs (Yang et al., 2023a; Team, 2023; Bai et al., 2023) of similar sizes but differing pre-trained models. By selecting these distinct groups, we aim to conduct a precise analysis across different versions and pre-trained models.

Various experiments indicate that LLMs possess a wealth of disciplinary knowledge and can handle questions, yet they remain sensitive to variations like different option orders and altered question descriptions, particularly the latter.

[1]https://github.com/THUDM/ChatGLM-6B
[2]https://github.com/thudm/chatglm2-6b
[3]https://github.com/THUDM/ChatGLM3

Our main contributions in the paper are as follows:

- We reassess the progress of Chinese LLMs in disciplinary knowledge and carry out a wide range of experiments to assess LLMs across various subject domains and educational levels.
- We devise six tasks, spanning from memorization detection to robustness, to explore the effects on each LLM. We have evaluated six advanced LLMs for two test groups based on their pre-training and timeline, leading to a comprehensive inquiry.
- Extensive experiments reveal that current LLMs have been exposed to a broad array of disciplinary questions and knowledge, yet they still lack a thorough grasp of such knowledge.

2 Related Work

Chinese LLM Benchmarks. Previous benchmarks (Guo et al., 2023; Liu et al., 2024b) for Chinese LLMs can be divided into four categories: discipline knowledge, general capabilities, safety, and special fields. Benchmarks for discipline knowledge (Huang et al., 2023; Liu et al., 2023a; Li et al., 2023; Gu et al., 2024; Liu et al., 2024a) are typically considered standardized measures for LLMs, as they often encompass various discipline-related questions gathered from human exams. In terms of general capabilities (Xu et al., 2023; Zeng et al., 2023b), current efforts focus on tasks like instruction-following (Jing et al., 2023), role-playing (Shen et al., 2023b), reasoning (He et al., 2021; Ge et al., 2021, 2022; Shi et al., 2024a; Liu et al., 2024c; Yu et al., 2024), and tool-learning (Ruan et al., 2023). In terms of safety, researchers pay attention to two dimensions: red-teaming (Sun et al., 2023; Liu et al., 2023b; Zhang et al., 2023b) and AI safety. Specifically, red-teaming involves researchers collecting prompts that could potentially lead LLMs to produce undesirable content, while the AI safety benchmark (Perez et al., 2023; Shi and Xiong, 2024) aims to identify LLMs' behaviors such as power-seeking (Hadshar, 2023). Benchmarks in special fields evaluate LLMs in various professional contexts, such as health (Wang et al., 2023), coding (Fu et al., 2023), law (Fei et al., 2023; Dai et al., 2024), and finance (Zhang et al., 2023a).

Task	Input	Output
1	Question	A:text, B:text, C:text, D:text
2	Question + A:	text, B:text, C:text, D:text
3	Question + A:text + B:text	C:text, D:text
4	Demonstrations + Question	A:text, B:text, C:text, D:text

Table 1: Different compositions of input and output in the memorization accessing task. Demonstrations are a sample of question and four options. In this paper, the number of demonstration is set to two.

In this paper, we focus on benchmarks with disciplinary knowledge for two primary reasons. Firstly, these benchmarks cover a variety of subjects, leading to a thorough assessment. Secondly, benchmarks of this nature are commonly used as the standard evaluation in LLM publications. Therefore, we have chosen M3KE (Liu et al., 2023a) as our testbed due to its wide coverage of questions and subjects.

Data Contamination. Despite the abundance of benchmarks assessing various capabilities of LLMs, a concerning trend is the ease with which public benchmarks are utilized to train subsequent LLMs. Ongoing efforts are aimed at addressing this issue (Sainz et al., 2023).

In terms of accessing contamination, a method proposed by researchers aims to determine whether content has been trained during the pre-training stage. Another method introduced by a different group Oren et al. (2023) involves constructing a statistical test for assessing testset contamination. One study focuses on an LLM-based decontamination method that can identify leaked texts even after being rewritten and translated (Yang et al., 2023b). Another investigation (Deng et al., 2023) delves into data contamination by measuring the overlap between target benchmarks and pre-training corpora, as well as masking incorrect options that may lead LLMs to make inaccurate predictions. Furthermore, researchers have developed detection pipelines to enhance benchmark transparency through search engines (Li et al., 2024) and metrics (Xu et al., 2024), proposing a new metric for evaluating memorization in LLMs (Schwarzschild et al., 2024).

Additional efforts are dedicated to exploring challenges within current benchmarks (Zhou et al., 2023; Carlini et al., 2023). One study (Zheng et al., 2023) examines the evolutionary trajectory of GPT, investigating whether the inclusion of code data enhances LLMs' reasoning abilities. Another research (Li and Flanigan, 2024) demonstrates a correlation between the performance of LLMs on benchmarks and their release dates. Moreover, other works explore the sensitivity of LLMs leaderboards (Alzahrani et al., 2024) and evaluate large vision-language models (Chen et al., 2024).

Drawing inspiration from these studies, our research focuses on the development of Chinese LLMs on discipline knowledge. This entails not only enhancing the retention of knowledge in LLMs based on the same pre-trained model, leading to a clear depiction of their evolution, but also evaluating the robustness of LLMs in terms of comprehension and mastery of knowledge.

3 Methodology

Concerning memorization, there are three further sub-dimensions. Initially, we employ a pre-training task to investigate the memorization capabilities of Chinese LLMs. Subsequently, we compare directly fine-tuning the earliest version of LLM released before M3KE, utilized in this paper, with other LLMs. Finally, we eliminate each question from the input, providing only four options to the LLMs, to assess whether they can offer correct answers without the question. For robustness, we randomize the order of options and rewrite questions separately, yielding a different perspective.

3.1 Assessing Memorization

In this section, we aim to investigate whether the development of Chinese LLMs is influenced by memorizing more data, such as QA pairs. To do this, we selected the ChatGLM-6B family as our experimental group, which includes ChatGLM1-6B, ChatGLM2-6B, and ChatGLM3-6B, released in chronological order. ChatGLM1-6B was released before M3KE, while ChatGLM2-6B and ChatGLM3-6B were released after it. We employed three methods to detect memorization: question-options completion, contaminational fine-tuning, and removal questions.

In the question-options completion, each question and its options are considered as sequential text, split into two parts: the input and the reference. LLMs are expected to provide predictions based on the input and the prompt, which are then compared against the reference. For instance, a question serves as the input, while the concatenation of its four options forms the reference. By crafting inputs, as illustrated in Table 1, we prompt the LLM to generate four new options based on

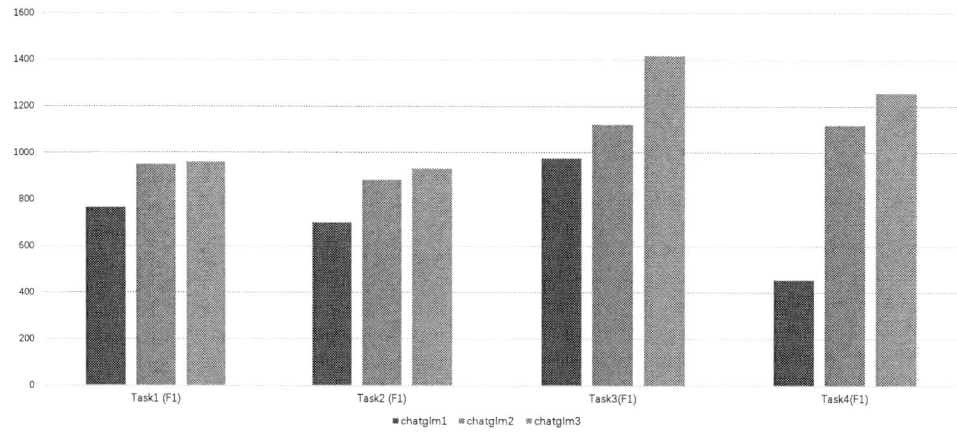

Figure 1: Results of question-options completion under different task settings.

the input. Evaluating the prediction against the reference, a higher F1 match rate indicates more memorization within the LLM. However, at times, the LLM may answer the question directly instead of following the instruction. To address this, we conducted this set of experiments under various settings, encompassing five tasks.

For the contaminational fine-tuning, we aim to investigate the impact of fine-tuning on the benchmark used to evaluate the LLM. Specifically, we fine-tune ChatGLM1-6B, the earliest released LLM in the ChatGLM-6B series on M3KE, with varying percentages (20%, 40%, 60%, 80%, and 100%) for comparison with ChatGLM2-6B and ChatGLM3-6B. Although there is no conclusive evidence of shared training data among the different LLM versions, it raises questions about potential contamination.

In removal questions scenario, we present four options to the LLM without any accompanying questions. Based on the hypothesis that if the LLM truly memorizes information, it should consistently select the correct option even without a specific question, as it would have retained various benchmark features, including the relationship between the correct option and the others.

3.2 Assessing Robustness

There are three sub-methods to explore the robustness of LLMs: shuffling the order of options, rewriting questions, and a combination of both.

In the task of shuffling options order, we shuffled the original order of four options, and each LLM is re-evaluated. Results in a new benchmark comprising original questions and options presented in a different order.

For rewriting questions, GPT-4 is tasked with rephrasing each question, providing a new description for the original question. Consequently, this benchmark includes new questions and options while maintaining the original order.

In the last task, the benchmark involves rewriting questions and rearranging options.

4 Experiments

We conducted extensive experiments to re-evaluate Chinese LLMs from the perspectives of memorization and robustness.

4.1 Settings

In our experiments, assessed these two aspects though the evolution of a LLM family including ChatGLM1-6B, ChatGLM2-6B and ChatGLM3-6B, resulting in a more precise description with data leakge. Besides, we added three Chinese LLMs, such as Baichuan2-7B-Chat, InternLM-7B-Chat and Qwen-7B-Chat, to identify current progresses in robustness. All of LLMs are trained by SFT/RLHF, which is able to follow instruction as well under the zero-shot setting.

For the test data, we used M3KE (Liu et al., 2023a) as our testbed due to its question consisting of multi-subjects and major Chinese education levels. This benchmark comprises 20,477 questions from 71 tasks gathered from authentic Chinese exams, aligning with the objectives of our study.

In addition, F1 was used as the main metric for the task of question-options completion and accuracy was adopted as the main evaluation metric for other tasks.

4.2 Results of Memorization

We accessed three LLMs from ChatGLM-6B series on the question-options completion task and con-

Cluster	Types	ChatGLM1-6B	ChatGLM2-6B	ChatGLM3-6B	InternLM-7B	Baichuan2-7B	Qwen-7B
A & H	Original	0.308	0.478	0.49	0.568	0.524	0.546
	Without Q	0.269	0.283	0.272	0.273	0.264	0.288
	Gaps	**0.039**	**0.195**	**0.218**	**0.295**	**0.26**	**0.258**
SS	Original	0.365	0.532	0.572	0.586	0.599	0.612
	Without Q	0.279	0.289	0.284	0.294	0.278	0.305
	Gaps	**0.086**	**0.243**	**0.288**	**0.292**	**0.321**	**0.307**
NS	Original	0.255	0.452	0.443	0.45	0.427	0.457
	Without Q	0.277	0.271	0.255	0.276	0.241	0.27
	Gaps	**-0.022**	**0.181**	**0.188**	**0.174**	**0.186**	**0.187**
OS	Original	0.343	0.468	0.518	0.543	0.54	0.543
	Without Q	0.269	0.259	0.271	0.258	0.238	0.26
	Gaps	**0.074**	**0.209**	**0.247**	**0.285**	**0.302**	**0.283**
PS	Original	0.26	0.407	0.454	0.528	0.407	0.465
	Without Q	0.235	0.311	0.297	0.269	0.287	0.244
	Gaps	**0.025**	**0.096**	**0.157**	**0.259**	**0.12**	**0.221**
MS	Original	0.323	0.639	0.587	0.604	0.497	0.563
	Without Q	0.264	0.276	0.263	0.305	0.267	0.297
	Gaps	**0.059**	**0.363**	**0.324**	**0.299**	**0.23**	**0.266**
HS	Original	0.256	0.437	0.473	0.555	0.434	0.485
	Without Q	0.286	0.277	0.265	0.299	0.264	0.305
	Gaps	**-0.03**	**0.16**	**0.208**	**0.256**	**0.17**	**0.18**
C	Original	0.309	0.475	0.489	0.497	0.522	0.529
	Without Q	0.282	0.28	0.268	0.275	0.254	0.283
	Gaps	**0.027**	**0.195**	**0.221**	**0.222**	**0.268**	**0.246**
OE	Original	0.322	0.441	0.481	0.516	0.518	0.529
	Without Q	0.258	0.262	0.267	0.263	0.241	0.26
	Gaps	**0.064**	**0.179**	**0.214**	**0.253**	**0.277**	**0.269**

Table 2: Results of question removal. A & H: Arts & Humanities. SC: Social Sciences. NS: Natural Sciences. OS: Other Subjects. PS: Primary School. JHS: Junior High School. HS: High School. C: College. OE: Other Education. InternLM-7B: InternLM-7B-Chat. Baichuan2-7B: Baichuan2-7B-Chat. Qwen-7B: Qwen-7B-Chat.

taminational fine-tuning task, which could provide evidences across the development of a LLM group. For question removal task, we added three LLMs from other model family to compare performance between original and revised results.

4.2.1 Task of Question-Options Completion

In this task, we divided each question and its four options into two parts using the next-token prediction method. We then presented the first part and task LLMs with predicting the remaining part. In the zero-shot scenario, there is a noticeable trend of increasing F1 scores across the ChatGLM group. However, we have identified some biases in the zero-shot setup. For instance, in task3, the input is the question, and the instruction is to ask the LLM to provide four options based on the question. Yet, at times, the LLMs answer the question but do not adhere to the instruction. To address this, we have introduced alternative formats, as detailed in Table 1 for task3 and task4. Furthermore, in the few-shot setting, we added two demonstrations before the input to improve instruction adherence. The results, as depicted in Fig. 1, clearly demonstrate that the new version of ChatGLM retains more information than the previous version across various settings.

4.2.2 Task of Contaminational Fine-tuning

Additionally, we aim to simulate direct contamination for ChatGLM by fine-tuning the LLM on M3KE. Specifically, we selected ChatGLM1 as our contaminated LLM, fine-tuned with varying percentages of 20%, 40%, 60%, 80%, and 100%, resulting in a noticeable data leakage. Fig. 2 illustrates the performance of the fine-tuned ChatGLM1 compared to the original ChatGLM1, ChatGLM2, and ChatGLM3. The general trend shows an improvement in performance as more data from M3KE is included, although there are occasional local fluctuations during this process. Initially, we observe a decrease in the performance of ChatGLM1 when fine-tuned with 20% of the test data, followed by a continuous improvement until reaching 60%. Subsequently, ChatGLM1 fine-tuned with 80% of the data experiences a decline, which is then followed by an increase when using 100% of the data. However, even with the optimal results achieved by fine-tuning M3KE, ChatGLM1 still lags behind ChatGLM2 and ChatGLM3, although they are closely aligned and perform better than ChatGLM2 in certain educational contexts. This suggests the possibility of training and fine-tuning similar data in the next generation of LLMs, in-

Cluster	Types	ChatGLM1-6B	ChatGLM2-6B	ChatGLM3-6B	InternLM-7B	Baichuan2-7B	Qwen-7B
	Original	0.308	0.478	0.49	0.568	0.524	0.546
A & H	revised	0.302	0.458	0.473	0.532	0.446	0.504
	Gaps	**0.006**	**0.02**	**0.017**	**0.036**	**0.078**	**0.042**
	Original	0.365	0.532	0.572	0.586	0.599	0.612
SS	revised	0.298	0.534	0.559	0.546	0.541	0.569
	Gaps	**0.067**	**-0.002**	**0.013**	**0.04**	**0.058**	**0.043**
	Original	0.255	0.452	0.443	0.45	0.427	0.457
NS	revised	0.283	0.451	0.427	0.439	0.393	0.441
	Gaps	**-0.028**	**0.001**	**0.016**	**0.011**	**0.034**	**0.016**
	Original	0.343	0.468	0.518	0.543	0.54	0.543
OS	revised	0.294	0.473	0.484	0.51	0.471	0.498
	Gaps	**0.049**	**-0.005**	**0.034**	**0.033**	**0.069**	**0.045**
	Original	0.26	0.407	0.454	0.528	0.407	0.465
PS	revised	0.324	0.409	0.389	0.474	0.314	0.451
	Gaps	**-0.064**	**-0.002**	**0.065**	**0.054**	**0.093**	**0.014**
	Original	0.323	0.639	0.587	0.604	0.497	0.563
MS	revised	0.309	0.596	0.572	0.629	0.466	0.579
	Gaps	**0.014**	**0.043**	**0.015**	**-0.025**	**0.031**	**-0.016**
	Original	0.256	0.437	0.473	0.555	0.434	0.485
HS	revised	0.278	0.476	0.458	0.503	0.4	0.463
	Gaps	**-0.022**	**-0.039**	**0.015**	**0.052**	**0.034**	**0.022**
	Original	0.309	0.475	0.489	0.497	0.522	0.529
C	revised	0.287	0.471	0.479	0.47	0.468	0.492
	Gaps	**0.022**	**0.004**	**0.01**	**0.027**	**0.054**	**0.037**
	Original	0.322	0.441	0.481	0.516	0.518	0.529
OE	revised	0.302	0.442	0.444	0.479	0.451	0.48
	Gaps	**0.02**	**-0.001**	**0.037**	**0.037**	**0.067**	**0.049**

Table 3: Results of shuffling the order of options. A & H: Arts & Humanities. SC: Social Sciences. NS: Natural Sciences. OS: Other Subjects. PS: Primary School. JHS: Junior High School. HS: High School. C: College. OE: Other Education. InternLM-7B: InternLM-7B-Chat. Baichuan2-7B: Baichuan2-7B-Chat. Qwen-7B: Qwen-7B-Chat.

Cluster	Types	ChatGLM1-6B	ChatGLM2-6B	ChatGLM3-6B	InternLM-7B	Baichuan2-7B	Qwen-7B
	Original	0.308	0.478	0.49	0.568	0.524	0.546
A & H	revised	0.298	0.359	0.364	0.439	0.293	0.392
	Gaps	**0.01**	**0.119**	**0.126**	**0.129**	**0.231**	**0.154**
	Original	0.365	0.532	0.572	0.586	0.599	0.612
SS	revised	0.331	0.414	0.397	0.439	0.335	0.424
	Gaps	**0.034**	**0.118**	**0.175**	**0.147**	**0.264**	**0.188**
	Original	0.255	0.452	0.443	0.45	0.427	0.457
NS	revised	0.313	0.381	0.323	0.373	0.286	0.374
	Gaps	**-0.058**	**0.071**	**0.12**	**0.077**	**0.141**	**0.083**
	Original	0.343	0.468	0.518	0.543	0.54	0.543
OS	revised	0.315	0.354	0.367	0.384	0.286	0.373
	Gaps	**0.028**	**0.114**	**0.151**	**0.159**	**0.254**	**0.17**
	Original	0.26	0.407	0.454	0.528	0.407	0.465
PS	revised	0.259	0.334	0.349	0.398	0.266	0.309
	Gaps	**0.001**	**0.073**	**0.105**	**0.13**	**0.141**	**0.156**
	Original	0.323	0.639	0.587	0.604	0.497	0.563
MS	revised	0.326	0.455	0.387	0.494	0.325	0.443
	Gaps	**-0.003**	**0.184**	**0.2**	**0.11**	**0.172**	**0.12**
	Original	0.256	0.437	0.473	0.555	0.434	0.485
HS	revised	0.316	0.376	0.349	0.424	0.3	0.387
	Gaps	**-0.06**	**0.061**	**0.124**	**0.131**	**0.134**	**0.098**
	Original	0.309	0.475	0.489	0.497	0.522	0.529
C	revised	0.319	0.388	0.355	0.389	0.307	0.392
	Gaps	**-0.01**	**0.087**	**0.134**	**0.108**	**0.215**	**0.137**
	Original	0.322	0.441	0.481	0.516	0.518	0.529
OE	revised	0.308	0.335	0.344	0.387	0.272	0.372
	Gaps	**0.014**	**0.106**	**0.137**	**0.129**	**0.246**	**0.157**

Table 4: Results of rewriting questions. A & H: Arts & Humanities. SC: Social Sciences. NS: Natural Sciences. OS: Other Subjects. PS: Primary School. JHS: Junior High School. HS: High School. C: College. OE: Other Education. InternLM-7B: InternLM-7B-Chat. Baichuan2-7B: Baichuan2-7B-Chat. Qwen-7B: Qwen-7B-Chat.

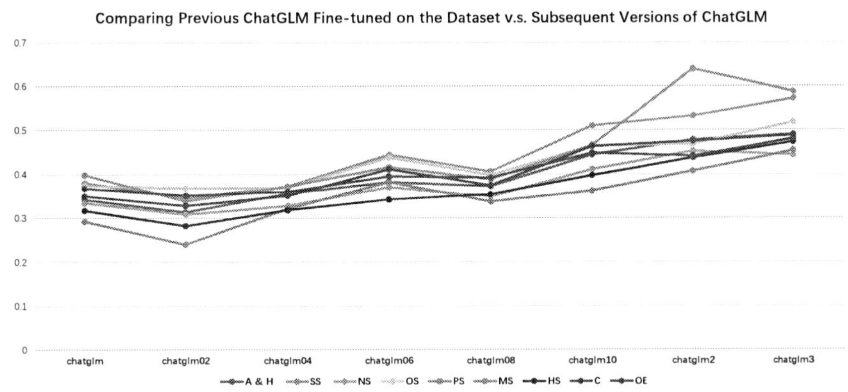

Figure 2: The results of contaminational fine-tuning. A & H: Arts & Humanities. SC: Social Sciences. NS: Natural Sciences. O: Other.

dicating that the development of training LLMs should incorporate more knowledge than previous versions, including insights from human evolution.

4.2.3 Task of Removal Questions

This task is designed to test whether the LLM can provide the correct answer without the question if it has been trained on question-answering pairs. We assessed six Chinese LLMs in M3KE, and the results are presented in Table 2. Most LLMs were impacted by this task, but ChatGLM1 appears to perform well, with even higher accuracy in two clusters than before. This suggests that ChatGLM1 might have been trained on multiple-choice questions related to those clusters in M3KE, specifically focusing on Nature Science at the subject level and High School at the education level. As ChatGLM versions progress, the impact on ChatGLM2 and ChatGLM3 becomes more pronounced, leading to a significant decrease in performance. This indicates that the training data for the later versions of ChatGLM may not contain the same questions as those in M3KE. Similarly, other LLMs like InternLM-7B-Chat, Baichuan2-7B-Chat, and Qwen-7B-Chat show a similar trend to ChatGLM2 and ChatGLM3. While it appears that newer LLMs may be predicting answers based on the questions rather than relying solely on memorization, it does not necessarily mean that the training data for these newer models lacks such knowledge.

The following question is whether LLMs effectively handle this knowledge? In other words, if LLMs truly master this knowledge, they should be able to address these questions across various scenarios. Consequently, we applied M3KE to different versions to assess the robustness of LLMs in the subsequent section.

4.3 Results of Robustness

In this section, we seek to assess the robustness of LLMs by modifying M3KE. This includes altering the sequence of options and rephrasing the original question. The core hypothesis here is that if an LLM comprehends the information, it should deliver comparable results with the unaltered test data. Hence, we adjusted M3KE using three approaches: rearranging option sequences, rephrasing questions, and combining shuffled options with rewritten questions. Furthermore, we introduce three LLMs from different companies in this segment - specifically InternLM-7B-Chat, Baichuan2-7B-Chat, and Qwen-7B-Chat - all of which exhibit impressive performance on M3KE.

4.3.1 Results of Shuffling the Order of Options

Table 3 shows the difference between the original and revised results on M3KE. The most significant decrease is observed at the primary school level for ChatGLM3, InternLM-7B-Chat, Baichuan2-7B-Chat, and Qwen-7B-Chat. Additionally, these language models, except for Baichuan2-7B-Chat, demonstrate relatively consistent performance in social science and natural science at the subject level, as well as in middle school, high school, and college at the education level. The largest deviation of 0.052 is seen in high school by InternLM-7B-Chat. Notably, ChatGLM2 remains consistent in this task, with only four cluster results decreasing.

Cluster	Types	ChatGLM1-6B	ChatGLM2-6B	ChatGLM3-6B	InternLM-7B	Baichuan2-7B	Qwen-7B
	Original	0.308	0.478	0.49	0.568	0.524	0.546
A & H	revised	0.303	0.353	0.364	0.426	0.298	0.366
	Gaps	**0.005**	**0.125**	**0.126**	**0.142**	**0.226**	**0.18**
	Original	0.365	0.532	0.572	0.586	0.599	0.612
SS	revised	0.315	0.386	0.384	0.421	0.319	0.409
	Gaps	**0.05**	**0.146**	**0.188**	**0.165**	**0.28**	**0.203**
	Original	0.255	0.452	0.443	0.45	0.427	0.457
NS	revised	0.288	0.353	0.32	0.356	0.286	0.355
	Gaps	**-0.033**	**0.099**	**0.123**	**0.094**	**0.141**	**0.102**
	Original	0.343	0.468	0.518	0.543	0.54	0.543
OS	revised	0.295	0.355	0.337	0.389	0.277	0.361
	Gaps	**0.048**	**0.113**	**0.181**	**0.154**	**0.263**	**0.182**
	Original	0.26	0.407	0.454	0.528	0.407	0.465
PS	revised	0.306	0.298	0.293	0.389	0.231	0.349
	Gaps	**-0.046**	**0.109**	**0.161**	**0.139**	**0.176**	**0.116**
	Original	0.323	0.639	0.587	0.604	0.497	0.563
MS	revised	0.307	0.433	0.392	0.492	0.313	0.404
	Gaps	**0.016**	**0.206**	**0.195**	**0.112**	**0.184**	**0.159**
	Original	0.256	0.437	0.473	0.555	0.434	0.485
HS	revised	0.282	0.382	0.336	0.392	0.292	0.36
	Gaps	**-0.026**	**0.055**	**0.137**	**0.163**	**0.142**	**0.125**
	Original	0.309	0.475	0.489	0.497	0.522	0.529
C	revised	0.3	0.352	0.348	0.374	0.304	0.376
	Gaps	**0.009**	**0.123**	**0.141**	**0.123**	**0.218**	**0.153**
	Original	0.322	0.441	0.481	0.516	0.518	0.529
OE	revised	0.298	0.352	0.336	0.378	0.277	0.355
	Gaps	**0.024**	**0.089**	**0.145**	**0.138**	**0.241**	**0.174**

Table 5: Results of combining rewritten questions and shuffled options. A & H: Arts & Humanities. SC: Social Sciences. NS: Natural Sciences. OS: Other Subjects. PS: Primary School. JHS: Junior High School. HS: High School. C: College. OE: Other Education. InternLM-7B: InternLM-7B-Chat. Baichuan2-7B: Baichuan2-7B-Chat. Qwen-7B: Qwen-7B-Chat.

4.3.2 Results of Rewriting Questions

Table 4 shows the performance impact of rewriting each question through prompting GPT-4. Compared to the previous method, we observe significant effects on most language models, particularly those excelling in original questions and released post M3KE. Within the ChatGLM category, the decline corresponds with the ChatGLM version, with ChatGLM3-6B, the latest model, experiencing the most reduction. ChatGLM1-6B, publicly available before M3KE, demonstrates similar performance. Notably, Baichuan2-7B-Chat appears to struggle with the modified questions, with the largest decrease of 0.264 in the social science cluster. InternLM-7B-Chat and Qwen-7B-Chat exhibit the most substantial reductions in other subject clusters and social science, with reductions of 0.159 and 0.188, respectively. Regarding educational levels, the most significant decreases are seen in other subjects for Baichuan2-7B-Chat and Qwen-7B-Chat, and in high school for InternLM-7B-Chat.

4.3.3 Results of Rewriting Questions with Shuffled Options

We merged the two tasks above, creating a benchmark with rewritten questions and reorganized option orders. This approach aligns with the task of question rewriting, as indicated in Table 5. It implies that existing Chinese LLMs are more attuned to the question descriptions than to the rearranged options, leading to observations that stronger LLMs might be trained with more structured questions, yet they may not grasp such knowledge types effectively. This indicates a need to reconsider the current advancements of Chinese LLMs focused on disciplinary knowledge benchmarks and prioritize robustness over ultimate performance.

5 Conclusion

In this paper, we have conducted a series of experiments to explore current progresses of Chinese LLMs on the discipline knowledge benchmark. We evaluated six Chinese SFT/RLHF LLMs belong to different groups to whether the new generation LLM memories more knowledge than the previous one, and the LLM taking more knowledge is able to handle those questions with different descriptions. Experiment results suggest although the newer LLM memorizes more knowledge, it still struggles with variations on the question, especially the description of question has more impact on LLMs.

Given that data contamination may pervade across different dimensions of LLM evaluation, we are keen to encourage the community further investigate current performance on public benchmarks.

Ethics Statement

The research process adheres strictly to the ACL Ethics Policy. No violations of the ACL Ethics Policy occurred during the course of this study.

Acknowledgements

The present research was partially supported by the National Key Research and Development Program of China (Grant No. 2023YFE0116400). Chuang Liu is also supported by China Scholarship Council (No.202106250144). We would like to thank the anonymous reviewers for their insightful comments.

References

Norah Alzahrani, Hisham Abdullah Alyahya, Yazeed Alnumay, Sultan Alrashed, Shaykhah Alsubaie, Yusef Almushaykeh, Faisal Mirza, Nouf Alotaibi, Nora Al-Twairesh, Areeb Alowisheq, M. Saiful Bari, and Haidar Khan. 2024. When benchmarks are targets: Revealing the sensitivity of large language model leaderboards. *CoRR*, abs/2402.01781.

Jinze Bai, Shuai Bai, Yunfei Chu, Zeyu Cui, Kai Dang, Xiaodong Deng, Yang Fan, Wenbin Ge, Yu Han, Fei Huang, Binyuan Hui, Luo Ji, Mei Li, Junyang Lin, Runji Lin, Dayiheng Liu, Gao Liu, Chengqiang Lu, Keming Lu, Jianxin Ma, Rui Men, Xingzhang Ren, Xuancheng Ren, Chuanqi Tan, Sinan Tan, Jianhong Tu, Peng Wang, Shijie Wang, Wei Wang, Shengguang Wu, Benfeng Xu, Jin Xu, An Yang, Hao Yang, Jian Yang, Shusheng Yang, Yang Yao, Bowen Yu, Hongyi Yuan, Zheng Yuan, Jianwei Zhang, Xingxuan Zhang, Yichang Zhang, Zhenru Zhang, Chang Zhou, Jingren Zhou, Xiaohuan Zhou, and Tianhang Zhu. 2023. Qwen technical report. *CoRR*, abs/2309.16609.

Nicholas Carlini, Daphne Ippolito, Matthew Jagielski, Katherine Lee, Florian Tramèr, and Chiyuan Zhang. 2023. Quantifying memorization across neural language models. In *The Eleventh International Conference on Learning Representations, ICLR 2023, Kigali, Rwanda, May 1-5, 2023*. OpenReview.net.

Lin Chen, Jinsong Li, Xiaoyi Dong, Pan Zhang, Yuhang Zang, Zehui Chen, Haodong Duan, Jiaqi Wang, Yu Qiao, Dahua Lin, and Feng Zhao. 2024. Are we on the right way for evaluating large vision-language models? *CoRR*, abs/2403.20330.

Yongfu Dai, Duanyu Feng, Jimin Huang, Haochen Jia, Qianqian Xie, Yifang Zhang, Weiguang Han, Wei Tian, and Hao Wang. 2024. LAiW: A chinese legal large language models benchmark.

Chunyuan Deng, Yilun Zhao, Xiangru Tang, Mark Gerstein, and Arman Cohan. 2023. Investigating data contamination in modern benchmarks for large language models. *CoRR*, abs/2311.09783.

Zhengxiao Du, Yujie Qian, Xiao Liu, Ming Ding, Jiezhong Qiu, Zhilin Yang, and Jie Tang. 2022. GLM: general language model pretraining with autoregressive blank infilling. In *Proceedings of the 60th Annual Meeting of the Association for Computational Linguistics (Volume 1: Long Papers), ACL 2022, Dublin, Ireland, May 22-27, 2022*, pages 320–335. Association for Computational Linguistics.

Zhiwei Fei, Xiaoyu Shen, Dawei Zhu, Fengzhe Zhou, Zhuo Han, Songyang Zhang, Kai Chen, Zongwen Shen, and Jidong Ge. 2023. LawBench: Benchmarking legal knowledge of large language models.

Lingyue Fu, Huacan Chai, Shuang Luo, Kounianhua Du, Weiming Zhang, Longteng Fan, Jiayi Lei, Renting Rui, Jianghao Lin, Yuchen Fang, Yifan Liu, Jingkuan Wang, Siyuan Qi, Kangning Zhang, Weinan Zhang, and Yong Yu. 2023. CodeApex: A bilingual programming evaluation benchmark for large language models. *CoRR*, abs/2309.01940.

Huibin Ge, Chenxi Sun, Deyi Xiong, and Qun Liu. 2021. Chinese WPLC: A Chinese dataset for evaluating pretrained language models on word prediction given long-range context. In *Proceedings of the 2021 Conference on Empirical Methods in Natural Language Processing*, pages 3770–3778, Online and Punta Cana, Dominican Republic. Association for Computational Linguistics.

Huibin Ge, Xiaohu Zhao, Chuang Liu, Yulong Zeng, Qun Liu, and Deyi Xiong. 2022. TGEA 2.0: A large-scale diagnostically annotated dataset with benchmark tasks for text generation of pretrained language models. In *Advances in Neural Information Processing Systems 35: Annual Conference on Neural Information Processing Systems 2022, NeurIPS 2022, New Orleans, LA, USA, November 28 - December 9, 2022*.

Zhouhong Gu, Xiaoxuan Zhu, Haoning Ye, Lin Zhang, Jianchen Wang, Yixin Zhu, Sihang Jiang, Zhuozhi Xiong, Zihan Li, Weijie Wu, Qianyu He, Rui Xu, Wenhao Huang, Jingping Liu, Zili Wang, Shusen Wang, Weiguo Zheng, Hongwei Feng, and Yanghua Xiao. 2024. Xiezhi: An ever-updating benchmark for holistic domain knowledge evaluation. In *Thirty-Eighth AAAI Conference on Artificial Intelligence, AAAI 2024, Thirty-Sixth Conference on Innovative Applications of Artificial Intelligence, IAAI 2024, Fourteenth Symposium on Educational Advances in Artificial Intelligence, EAAI 2014, February 20-27, 2024, Vancouver, Canada*, pages 18099–18107. AAAI Press.

Zishan Guo, Renren Jin, Chuang Liu, Yufei Huang, Dan Shi, Supryadi, Linhao Yu, Yan Liu, Jiaxuan Li, Bojian Xiong, and Deyi Xiong. 2023. Evaluating large language models: A comprehensive survey. *CoRR*, abs/2310.19736.

Rose Hadshar. 2023. A review of the evidence for existential risk from AI via misaligned power-seeking. *CoRR*, abs/2310.18244.

Jie He, Bo Peng, Yi Liao, Qun Liu, and Deyi Xiong. 2021. TGEA: An error-annotated dataset and benchmark tasks for TextGeneration from pretrained language models. In *Proceedings of the 59th Annual Meeting of the Association for Computational Linguistics and the 11th International Joint Conference on Natural Language Processing (Volume 1: Long Papers)*, pages 6012–6025, Online. Association for Computational Linguistics.

Yufei Huang and Deyi Xiong. 2024. CBBQ: A Chinese bias benchmark dataset curated with human-AI collaboration for large language models. In *Proceedings of the 2024 Joint International Conference on Computational Linguistics, Language Resources and Evaluation (LREC-COLING 2024)*, pages 2917–2929, Torino, Italia. ELRA and ICCL.

Yuzhen Huang, Yuzhuo Bai, Zhihao Zhu, Junlei Zhang, Jinghan Zhang, Tangjun Su, Junteng Liu, Chuancheng Lv, Yikai Zhang, Jiayi Lei, Yao Fu, Maosong Sun, and Junxian He. 2023. C-Eval: A multi-level multi-discipline chinese evaluation suite for foundation models. In *Advances in Neural Information Processing Systems 36: Annual Conference on Neural Information Processing Systems 2023, NeurIPS 2023, New Orleans, LA, USA, December 10 - 16, 2023*.

Yimin Jing, Renren Jin, Jiahao Hu, Huishi Qiu, Xiaohua Wang, Peng Wang, and Deyi Xiong. 2023. Follow-Eval: A multi-dimensional benchmark for assessing the instruction-following capability of large language models. *CoRR*, abs/2311.09829.

Timo Kaufmann, Paul Weng, Viktor Bengs, and Eyke Hüllermeier. 2024. A survey of reinforcement learning from human feedback.

Changmao Li and Jeffrey Flanigan. 2024. Task Contamination: Language models may not be few-shot anymore. In *Thirty-Eighth AAAI Conference on Artificial Intelligence, AAAI 2024, Thirty-Sixth Conference on Innovative Applications of Artificial Intelligence, IAAI 2024, Fourteenth Symposium on Educational Advances in Artificial Intelligence, EAAI 2014, February 20-27, 2024, Vancouver, Canada*, pages 18471–18480. AAAI Press.

Haonan Li, Yixuan Zhang, Fajri Koto, Yifei Yang, Hai Zhao, Yeyun Gong, Nan Duan, and Timothy Baldwin. 2023. CMMLU: measuring massive multitask language understanding in chinese. *CoRR*, abs/2306.09212.

Yucheng Li, Frank Guerin, and Chenghua Lin. 2024. An open source data contamination report for large language models.

Chuang Liu, Renren Jin, Yuqi Ren, and Deyi Xiong. 2024a. LHMKE: A large-scale holistic multi-subject knowledge evaluation benchmark for Chinese large language models. In *Proceedings of the 2024 Joint International Conference on Computational Linguistics, Language Resources and Evaluation (LREC-COLING 2024)*, pages 10476–10487, Torino, Italia. ELRA and ICCL.

Chuang Liu, Renren Jin, Yuqi Ren, Linhao Yu, Tianyu Dong, Xiaohan Peng, Shuting Zhang, Jianxiang Peng, Peiyi Zhang, Qingqing Lyu, Xiaowen Su, Qun Liu, and Deyi Xiong. 2023a. M3KE: A massive multi-level multi-subject knowledge evaluation benchmark for chinese large language models. *CoRR*, abs/2305.10263.

Chuang Liu, Linhao Yu, Jiaxuan Li, Renren Jin, Yufei Huang, Ling Shi, Junhui Zhang, Xinmeng Ji, Tingting Cui, Liutao, Jinwang Song, Hongying ZAN, Sun Li, and Deyi Xiong. 2024b. OpenEval: Benchmarking chinese LLMs across capability, alignment and safety. In *ACL 2024 System Demonstration Track*.

Xiao Liu, Xuanyu Lei, Shengyuan Wang, Yue Huang, Zhuoer Feng, Bosi Wen, Jiale Cheng, Pei Ke, Yifan Xu, Weng Lam Tam, Xiaohan Zhang, Lichao Sun, Hongning Wang, Jing Zhang, Minlie Huang, Yuxiao Dong, and Jie Tang. 2023b. AlignBench: Benchmarking chinese alignment of large language models. *CoRR*, abs/2311.18743.

Yan Liu, Renren Jin, Lin Shi, Zheng Yao, and Deyi Xiong. 2024c. FineMath: A fine-grained mathematical evaluation benchmark for chinese large language models. *CoRR*, abs/2403.07747.

OpenAI. 2023. GPT-4 technical report. *CoRR*, abs/2303.08774.

Yonatan Oren, Nicole Meister, Niladri S. Chatterji, Faisal Ladhak, and Tatsunori B. Hashimoto. 2023. Proving test set contamination in black box language models. *CoRR*, abs/2310.17623.

Ethan Perez, Sam Ringer, Kamile Lukosiute, Karina Nguyen, Edwin Chen, Scott Heiner, Craig Pettit, Catherine Olsson, Sandipan Kundu, Saurav Kadavath, Andy Jones, Anna Chen, Benjamin Mann, Brian Israel, Bryan Seethor, Cameron McKinnon, Christopher Olah, Da Yan, Daniela Amodei, Dario Amodei, Dawn Drain, Dustin Li, Eli Tran-Johnson, Guro Khundadze, Jackson Kernion, James Landis, Jamie Kerr, Jared Mueller, Jeeyoon Hyun, Joshua Landau, Kamal Ndousse, Landon Goldberg, Liane Lovitt, Martin Lucas, Michael Sellitto, Miranda Zhang, Neerav Kingsland, Nelson Elhage, Nicholas Joseph, Noemí Mercado, Nova DasSarma, Oliver

Rausch, Robin Larson, Sam McCandlish, Scott Johnston, Shauna Kravec, Sheer El Showk, Tamera Lanham, Timothy Telleen-Lawton, Tom Brown, Tom Henighan, Tristan Hume, Yuntao Bai, Zac Hatfield-Dodds, Jack Clark, Samuel R. Bowman, Amanda Askell, Roger Grosse, Danny Hernandez, Deep Ganguli, Evan Hubinger, Nicholas Schiefer, and Jared Kaplan. 2023. Discovering language model behaviors with model-written evaluations. In *Findings of the Association for Computational Linguistics: ACL 2023, Toronto, Canada, July 9-14, 2023*, pages 13387–13434. Association for Computational Linguistics.

Jingqing Ruan, Yihong Chen, Bin Zhang, Zhiwei Xu, Tianpeng Bao, Guoqing Du, Shiwei Shi, Hangyu Mao, Ziyue Li, Xingyu Zeng, et al. 2023. TPTU: large language model-based ai agents for task planning and tool usage. *arXiv preprint arXiv:2308.03427*.

Oscar Sainz, Jon Ander Campos, Iker García-Ferrero, Julen Etxaniz, Oier Lopez de Lacalle, and Eneko Agirre. 2023. NLP evaluation in trouble: On the need to measure LLM data contamination for each benchmark. In *Findings of the Association for Computational Linguistics: EMNLP 2023, Singapore, December 6-10, 2023*, pages 10776–10787. Association for Computational Linguistics.

Avi Schwarzschild, Zhili Feng, Pratyush Maini, Zachary C Lipton, and J Zico Kolter. 2024. Rethinking llm memorization through the lens of adversarial compression. *arXiv preprint arXiv:2404.15146*.

Tianhao Shen, Renren Jin, Yufei Huang, Chuang Liu, Weilong Dong, Zishan Guo, Xinwei Wu, Yan Liu, and Deyi Xiong. 2023a. Large language model alignment: A survey. *CoRR*, abs/2309.15025.

Tianhao Shen, Sun Li, and Deyi Xiong. 2023b. RoleEval: A bilingual role evaluation benchmark for large language models. *CoRR*, abs/2312.16132.

Dan Shi, Chaobin You, Jiantao Huang, Taihao Li, and Deyi Xiong. 2024a. CORECODE: A common sense annotated dialogue dataset with benchmark tasks for chinese large language models. In *Thirty-Eighth AAAI Conference on Artificial Intelligence, AAAI 2024, Thirty-Sixth Conference on Innovative Applications of Artificial Intelligence, IAAI 2024, Fourteenth Symposium on Educational Advances in Artificial Intelligence, EAAI 2014, February 20-27, 2024, Vancouver, Canada*, pages 18952–18960. AAAI Press.

Ling Shi and Deyi Xiong. 2024. CRiskEval: A Chinese multi-level risk evaluation benchmark dataset for large language models. *arXiv preprint arXiv:2406.04752*.

Weijia Shi, Anirudh Ajith, Mengzhou Xia, Yangsibo Huang, Daogao Liu, Terra Blevins, Danqi Chen, and Luke Zettlemoyer. 2024b. Detecting pretraining data from large language models. In *The Twelfth International Conference on Learning Representations*.

Hao Sun, Zhexin Zhang, Jiawen Deng, Jiale Cheng, and Minlie Huang. 2023. Safety assessment of chinese large language models. *CoRR*, abs/2304.10436.

InternLM Team. 2023. InternLM: A multilingual language model with progressively enhanced capabilities. `https://github.com/InternLM/InternLM`.

Xidong Wang, Guiming Hardy Chen, Dingjie Song, Zhiyi Zhang, Zhihong Chen, Qingying Xiao, Feng Jiang, Jianquan Li, Xiang Wan, Benyou Wang, and Haizhou Li. 2023. CMB: A comprehensive medical benchmark in chinese. *CoRR*, abs/2308.08833.

Liang Xu, Anqi Li, Lei Zhu, Hang Xue, Changtai Zhu, Kangkang Zhao, Haonan He, Xuanwei Zhang, Qiyue Kang, and Zhenzhong Lan. 2023. SuperCLUE: A comprehensive chinese large language model benchmark. *CoRR*, abs/2307.15020.

Ruijie Xu, Zengzhi Wang, Run-Ze Fan, and Pengfei Liu. 2024. Benchmarking benchmark leakage in large language models. *arXiv preprint arXiv:2404.18824*.

Aiyuan Yang, Bin Xiao, Bingning Wang, Borong Zhang, Ce Bian, Chao Yin, Chenxu Lv, Da Pan, Dian Wang, Dong Yan, Fan Yang, Fei Deng, Feng Wang, Feng Liu, Guangwei Ai, Guosheng Dong, Haizhou Zhao, Hang Xu, Haoze Sun, Hongda Zhang, Hui Liu, Jiaming Ji, Jian Xie, Juntao Dai, Kun Fang, Lei Su, Liang Song, Lifeng Liu, Liyun Ru, Luyao Ma, Mang Wang, Mickel Liu, MingAn Lin, Nuolan Nie, Peidong Guo, Ruiyang Sun, Tao Zhang, Tianpeng Li, Tianyu Li, Wei Cheng, Weipeng Chen, Xiangrong Zeng, Xiaochuan Wang, Xiaoxi Chen, Xin Men, Xin Yu, Xuehai Pan, Yanjun Shen, Yiding Wang, Yiyu Li, Youxin Jiang, Yuchen Gao, Yupeng Zhang, Zenan Zhou, and Zhiying Wu. 2023a. Baichuan 2: Open large-scale language models. *CoRR*, abs/2309.10305.

Shuo Yang, Wei-Lin Chiang, Lianmin Zheng, Joseph E. Gonzalez, and Ion Stoica. 2023b. Rethinking benchmark and contamination for language models with rephrased samples. *CoRR*, abs/2311.04850.

Linhao Yu, Qun Liu, and Deyi Xiong. 2024. LFED: A literary fiction evaluation dataset for large language models. In *Proceedings of the 2024 Joint International Conference on Computational Linguistics, Language Resources and Evaluation (LREC-COLING 2024)*, pages 10466–10475, Torino, Italia. ELRA and ICCL.

Aohan Zeng, Xiao Liu, Zhengxiao Du, Zihan Wang, Hanyu Lai, Ming Ding, Zhuoyi Yang, Yifan Xu, Wendi Zheng, Xiao Xia, Weng Lam Tam, Zixuan Ma, Yufei Xue, Jidong Zhai, Wenguang Chen, Zhiyuan Liu, Peng Zhang, Yuxiao Dong, and Jie Tang. 2023a. GLM-130B: an open bilingual pre-trained model. In *The Eleventh International Conference on Learning Representations, ICLR 2023, Kigali, Rwanda, May 1-5, 2023*. OpenReview.net.

Hui Zeng, Jingyuan Xue, Meng Hao, Chen Sun, Bin Ning, and Na Zhang. 2023b. Evaluating the generation capabilities of large chinese language models. *CoRR*, abs/2308.04823.

Liwen Zhang, Weige Cai, Zhaowei Liu, Zhi Yang, Wei Dai, Yujie Liao, Qianru Qin, Yifei Li, Xingyu Liu, Zhiqiang Liu, Zhoufan Zhu, Anbo Wu, Xin Guo, and Yun Chen. 2023a. FinEval: A chinese financial domain knowledge evaluation benchmark for large language models. *CoRR*, abs/2308.09975.

Shengyu Zhang, Linfeng Dong, Xiaoya Li, Sen Zhang, Xiaofei Sun, Shuhe Wang, Jiwei Li, Runyi Hu, Tianwei Zhang, Fei Wu, and Guoyin Wang. 2024. Instruction tuning for large language models: A survey.

Zhexin Zhang, Leqi Lei, Lindong Wu, Rui Sun, Yongkang Huang, Chong Long, Xiao Liu, Xuanyu Lei, Jie Tang, and Minlie Huang. 2023b. SafetyBench: Evaluating the safety of large language models with multiple choice questions. *CoRR*, abs/2309.07045.

Wayne Xin Zhao, Kun Zhou, Junyi Li, Tianyi Tang, Xiaolei Wang, Yupeng Hou, Yingqian Min, Beichen Zhang, Junjie Zhang, Zican Dong, Yifan Du, Chen Yang, Yushuo Chen, Zhipeng Chen, Jinhao Jiang, Ruiyang Ren, Yifan Li, Xinyu Tang, Zikang Liu, Peiyu Liu, Jian-Yun Nie, and Ji-Rong Wen. 2023. A survey of large language models.

Shen Zheng, Yuyu Zhang, Yijie Zhu, Chenguang Xi, Pengyang Gao, Xun Zhou, and Kevin Chen-Chuan Chang. 2023. GPT-Fathom: Benchmarking large language models to decipher the evolutionary path towards GPT-4 and beyond. *CoRR*, abs/2309.16583.

Kun Zhou, Yutao Zhu, Zhipeng Chen, Wentong Chen, Wayne Xin Zhao, Xu Chen, Yankai Lin, Ji-Rong Wen, and Jiawei Han. 2023. Don't make your LLM an evaluation benchmark cheater. *CoRR*, abs/2311.01964.

Confounders in Instance Variation for the Analysis of Data Contamination

Behzad Mehrbakhsh[a,b,c;*], **Darío Garigliotti**[d],
Fernando Martínez-Plumed[a,b] and **José Hernández-Orallo**[a,b,c]
[a]UPV - Universitat Politècnica de València
[b]VRAIN - Valencian Research Institute for Artificial Intelligence
[c]ValgrAI - Valencian Graduate School and Research Network of Artificial Intelligence
[d]UiB - University of Bergen

Abstract

Test contamination is a serious problem for the evaluation of large language models (LLMs) because it leads to the overestimation of their performance and a quick saturation of benchmarks, even before the actual capability is achieved. One strategy to address this issue is the (adversarial) generation of variations, by including different exemplars and different rephrasings of the questions. However, these two interventions can lead to instances that can be more difficult (accumulating on the expected loss of performance by partly removing the contamination) but also to instances that can be less difficult (cancelling the expected loss of performance), which would make contamination undetectable. Understanding these two phenomena in terms of instance difficulty is critical to determine and measure contamination. In this paper we conduct a comprehensive analysis of these two interventions on an addition task with fine-tuned LLAMA-2 models.

1 Introduction

Large Language Models (LLMs) (Brown et al., 2020) have transformed Natural Language processing, but face evaluation challenges, especially with publicly available benchmarks. A key issue is *data contamination* (Ravaut et al., 2024), where training data contains test instances. A model trained on this data has seen part of the test set, which can have important effects in the evaluation of the model, leading to inflated performance measures (Yang et al., 2023; Sainz et al., 2023).

Recently, it has been seen that the actual issue of data contamination could be more predominant, as it is not only present by exact copies of the test instances in the training data. Studies such as the one by Yang et al. (2023) show that even rephrased or translated test instances in training data can improve performance, indicating potential contamination. However, the effect of the *difficulty* of these rephrased items has not been yet investigated. For instance, rephrasing can involve more convoluted or unusual expressions, which make the item more difficult for language models. Table 1 shows a series of *templates* that can be used to rephrase the expression behind the task of adding two numbers. The actual *exemplar* (the pair of $[term_1]$ and $[term_2]$) can also be replaced by a different pair to avoid contamination. These two interventions (different rephrasing or exemplar) can have mixed effects: some variations may inadvertently increase the difficulty of the instances, leading to an expected drop in performance, masking contamination, while others may make the instance easier and leading to an overestimation of performance, leading to false positives.

	Template
1	Can you please add $[term_1]$ and $[term_2]$ together?
2	Find the sum of $[term_1]$ and $[term_2]$.
3	Add up two numbers: $[term_1]$ and $[term_2]$.
4	Please work out the total of $[term_1]$ and $[term_2]$.
5	Please determine the numeric sum of $[term_1]$ and $[term_2]$.
6	Proceed to identify the aggregated total of the numbers $[term_1]$ and $[term_2]$.
7	Perform an addition operation on the numerical values $[term_1]$ and $[term_2]$.

Table 1: Various templates created by GPT-4 for the addition task. By instantiating them with different exemplars, we can get different instances, such as 'Find the sum of 56 and 723' and 'Perform an addition operation on the numerical values 35 and 85'. Are these two instances equally difficult?

Understanding these phenomena in terms of instance difficulty is a novel approach for accurately identifying and measuring contamination. In this study, we conduct a thorough analysis of rephrased templates and replaced exemplars using fine-tuned LLAMA-2 (Touvron et al., 2023) models for an

*Corresponding author. Email: bmehrba@upv.es .

Proceedings of the 1st Workshop on Data Contamination (CONDA), pages 13–21
August 16, 2024 ©2024 Association for Computational Linguistics

addition task. We generate templates of varying difficulty using GPT-4 (Achiam et al., 2023), fine-tune the models, and assess how these variations affect performance on exemplars of varying number of digits (and hence difficulty).

The main contributions are:

- We investigate how different rephrased and replaced test instances impact the performance of fine-tuned LLAMA-2 models on an addition task, revealing critical insights into the effects of data contamination.
- We study the impact of template difficulty on model performance, highlighting that variations in test instance phrasing can significantly affect evaluation outcomes.
- We evaluate the effects of fine-tuning with easy versus hard templates, showing how template diversity and intrinsic difficulty influence model performance and contamination detection.

The following sections detail our experimental design, methodology, and results.

2 Background

Several methods have been used to address data contamination. Prior to big tech companies close sourced their models and the training data, a common approach was trying to look for evaluation instances in the training data. String matching and embedding similarity are two techniques that have been commonly used for this purpose. OpenAI used 8-gram matching of test instances and training dataset for GPT-2 model (Radford et al., 2019). For GPT-3 (Brown et al., 2020) the same approach has been taken and all data points from the evaluation sets that had a 13-gram collision in the pre-training Common Crawl (C4) dataset were removed to tackle contamination.

As contamination can involve minor variations of the examples, calculating cosine similarity between embeddings of test and training items can also be used for finding cases in which the test item has been rephrased or expressed in a different language (Gunasekar et al., 2023) (Riddell et al., 2024).

But string matching and even embedding matching are not able detect rephrased test items effectively in general (Yang et al., 2023). More sophisticated and effective techniques employ embedding similarity search to identify the top-k samples similar to a given test sample and then prompting a powerful LLM such as GPT-4 to determine if any of the k samples are too similar to the test case.

For closed source models where no information regarding the training set is provided, none of the above mentioned methods are applicable. Introducing new contamination-free benchmarks such as LastEval (Li, 2023), WIKIMIA (Shi et al., 2023), KIEval (Yu et al., 2024), LiveCodeBench (Jain et al., 2024), Termite (Ranaldi et al., 2024) might seem a reliable solution for the problem, but as (Balloccu et al., 2024) mentioned, these new benchmarks can get contaminated as soon as they are publicly available or even just when used for evaluating closed source models by the creators of the benchmark themselves for the first time. In addition, building a high quality benchmark is a time consuming process and can not be done overnight.

Consequently, the idea of continuously generating new variation has taken ground. Clean-Eval (Zhu et al., 2023) intends to 'purify' current benchmarks by rephrasing the test items. While a drop in the performance of LLMs on the rephrased data points is considered as a sign of decontamination, the role of difficulty has been neglected in their analysis.

3 Methodology

Data contamination occurs when instances from the test set are found in the train set of AI models. For example, if a model is tested on the question "*What is 123 + 456?*" but has seen the same question (and answer) during training, it might simply recall the answer rather than 'compute' it again. Even if rephrased forms of test items like "*Calculate the sum of 123 and 456*" or "*What do you get when you add 456 to 123?*" exist in the training data, the evaluation is still compromised. These rephrased forms can inadvertently aid the model, causing an overestimation of its true capabilities.

On the other hand, testing on the rephrased form of original test items is suggested by the researchers to mitigate the contamination problem. Yet to the best of our knowledge, the role of difficulty of original test items and their variants has not been studied. Also, what matters more, the change in the exemplar or rephrasing the template? For instance, solving "*Find the result of 9876 + 54321*" might naturally be harder than "*Compute 12 + 34,*" regardless of rephrasing.

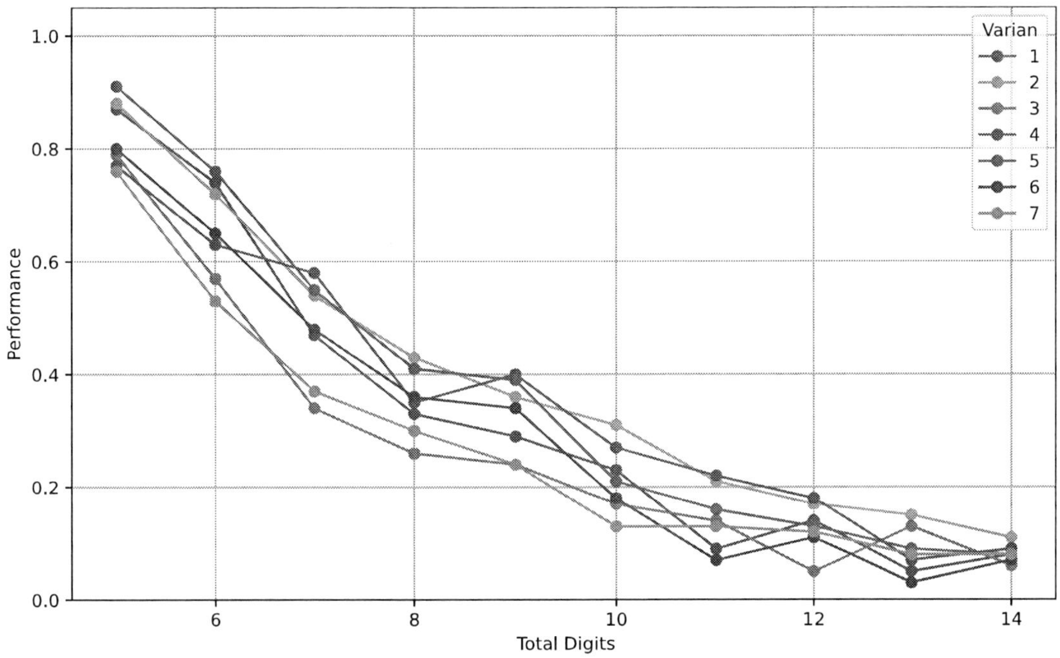

Figure 1: Performance of Llama2 7B chat model on the constructed dataset of addition.

Dataset Construction To explore these considerations, we designed a dataset of addition problems varying in complexity. Specifically, we generated 1,000 addition pairs (each different pair is an exemplar) for numbers ranging from five to fourteen digits. Each exemplar's intrinsic difficulty was determined by the sum of the number of digits of the addends. For example, the intrinsic difficulty of "829 + 4531" is 7.

Instance templates To produce varied instances, we asked GPT-4 to rephrase each addition problem in ten different ways. After excluding three ambiguous rephrasings, we used the remaining seven clear templates (see table 1). By applying seven templates to one thousand addition pairs, we generated seven thousand instances.

Model Evaluation and Fine-Tuning We used the Llama-2 7B chat model to check how different templates and exemplar affect model performance. First, we tested the model on the 7,000 instances (1,000 different exemplars per template) to get a baseline performance, as shown in Figure 1. We see some noticeable effect of the template (#2, orange, being much better than #7, pink), and a very significant influence of the #digits.

We performed three main fine-tuning experiments to explore how template variations affect model performance. In the first experiment, we used 70% of the exemplars (700), each with a different template, keeping a balanced representation of templates in the training data (equal number of exemplars, 100, for each template). The remaining 30% of the exemplars (300) was left for a non-contaminated validation set. Figure 2 shows the data construction process for our fist fine-tuning experiment.

The second experiment focused on the impact of template difficulty. We fine-tuned the model with either the easiest template (template 2) or the hardest template (template 7), based on initial performance evaluation (Figure 1). We then tested the fine-tuned models on all templates to see how this affected performance (Figure 5).

In the last experiment, we study the role of diversity of contaminating items. We compare the performance of the fine-tuned models when trained on four templates (#1, #2, #3 and #4) with the case only one of these templates is included in training, but repeated four times. (Figure 7)

In all cases we fine-tune Llama2 7B Chat model. Our fine-tuning process used the QLoRA method (Dettmers et al., 2024), implemented through the Huggingface pipeline. The choice of QLoRA allowed us to fit the entire Llama2 7B chat model within the memory constraints of a single NVIDIA

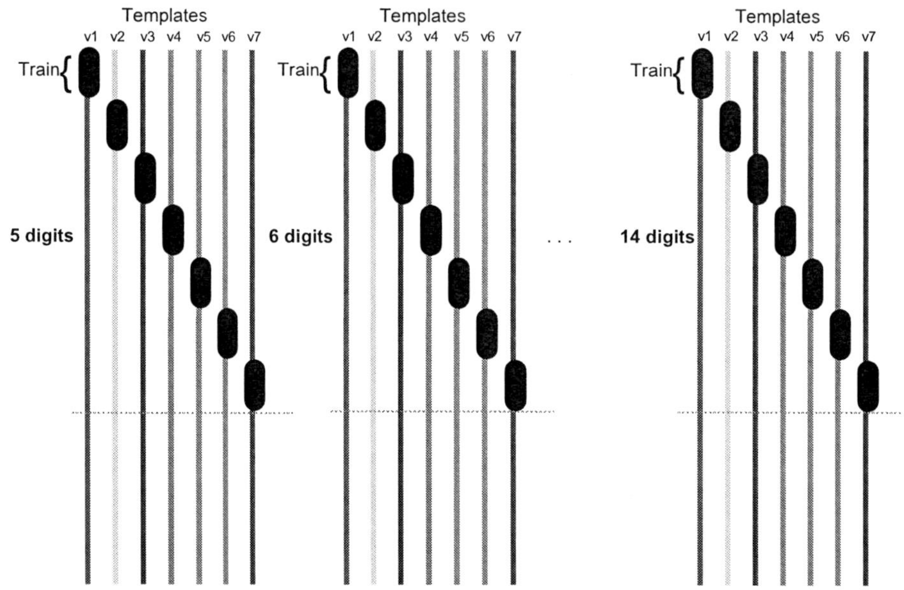

Figure 2: Data split for the first fine-tuning experiment. For each of the 10 digit lengths, 100 addition pairs (exemplars) are randomly generated. 70% are used for contaminating the training data. By applying 7 templates that are demonstrated with different colour in this figure, 490 instances can be created, one in seven (70) appearing in the train (shown in black) and the rest in the test. The 30 % of the original exemplars for this digit length are kept as non-contaminated validation set (below the dashed line) also with seven variations each in the test set (210).

GeForce RTX 3090 GPU with 24 gigabytes of RAM, making fine-tuning feasible for accessible hardware. The learning rate has been set to 1e-3 and batch size of 8 has been used. Through careful calibration, we found that this configuration provides an optimal balance, maximizing model performance while avoiding memory constraint issues. For the first and second experiments we fine-tuned the model for 5 epochs. For the third experiments 1 epoch is as the data is duplicated 4 times.

3.1 Research Questions

To guide our analysis, we formulated the following research questions, based on the first intervention (rephrasing):

1. **RQ1:** How does the difficulty of rephrased templates affect the performance of Llama-2 in the presence of potential data contamination?

2. **RQ2:** Does the performance of Llama-2 on contaminated data differ when fine-tuned to templates of different difficulty?

3. **RQ3:** What is the effect of varying the difficulty of the templates used for fine-tuning on the level of data contamination and the subsequent performance evaluation of Llama-2?

All these questions are analysed in the context of the exemplar difficulty as well (# digits), as this is the second intervention that can affect performance, and one intervention can mask the other:

4 Results

As shown in previous studies, LLMs are sensitive to prompts, i.e., the way that the request is formulated. Figure 1 shows that even for a simple task such as addition, rephrasing the question influences model performance. We can observe that template 2 in average is the easiest and template 7 is the most difficult version of rephrasing addition among our 7 templates. Consequently, as rephrasing a test item can change its difficulty level, this should be considered when this approach –rephrasing test items– is taken to address contamination. A lower performance of models on the rephrased test items might be simply due to the higher difficulty level of them and may not be a sign of their purity.

Figure 3 demonstrate this effect more clearly. As it can be seen, there are cases that the performance of the model for one or more templates when tested on the non-contaminated validation

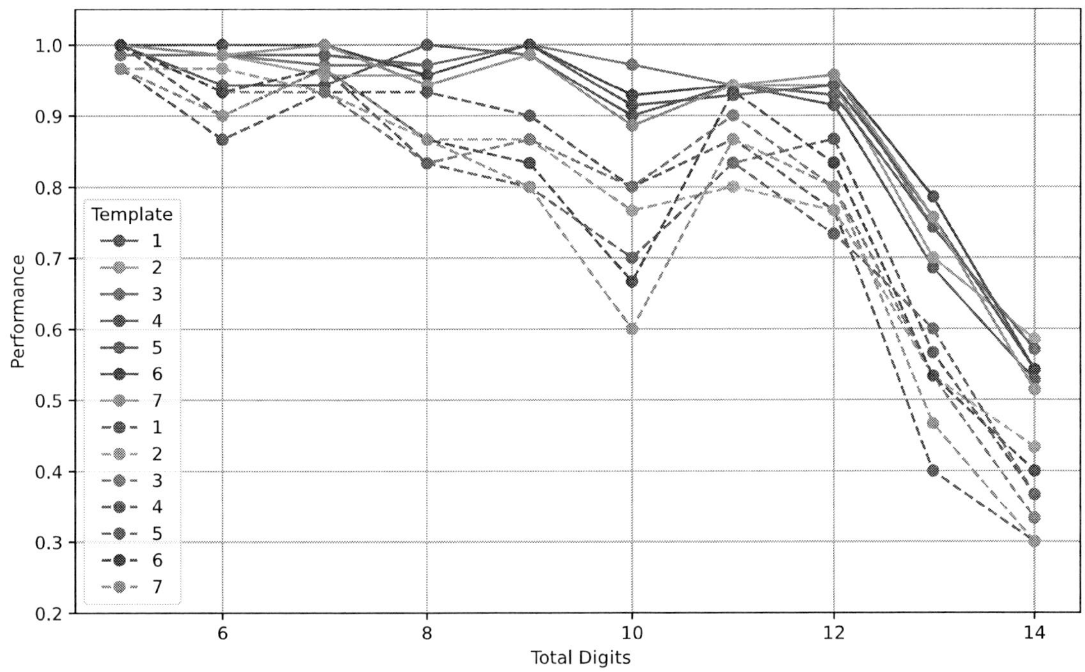

Figure 3: Performance of Llama2 7B chat model fine-tuned on the data described on Figure 2. The dashed lines show the performance of fine-tuned model on the contaminated test set. The test set is contaminated because it contains the exemplar (addition pairs) appeared in the training with the original template and the other 6 templates. The solid lines show the performance of the fine-tune model on the validation set where no exemplar (addition pair) from it exists in the training set.

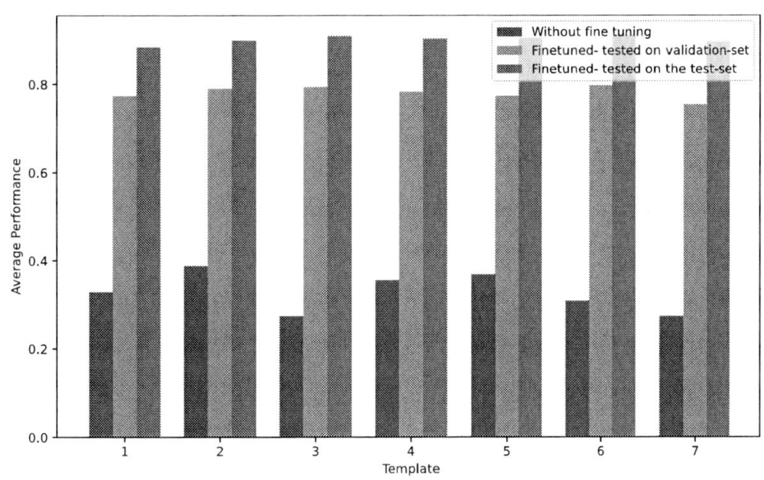

Figure 4: Llama2 7B model average performance comparison when tested on the non-contaminated validation-set, the contaminated test-set, train-set, and test-set excluding training instances

set is higher than some templates when tested on the contaminated test-set. This phenomenon can be seen for 5-digit, 6-digit, 7-digit, and 11-digit additions (Figure 3 clearly demonstrates this when the solid lines cross the dashed lines).

4.1 Difficulty of the Contaminating Template

Rephrased items that can potentially be found in the training data might have a different difficulty level compared to the test data points and can influence the contaminating level in different ways. To analyze this, we fine-tuned Llama2 7B chat model

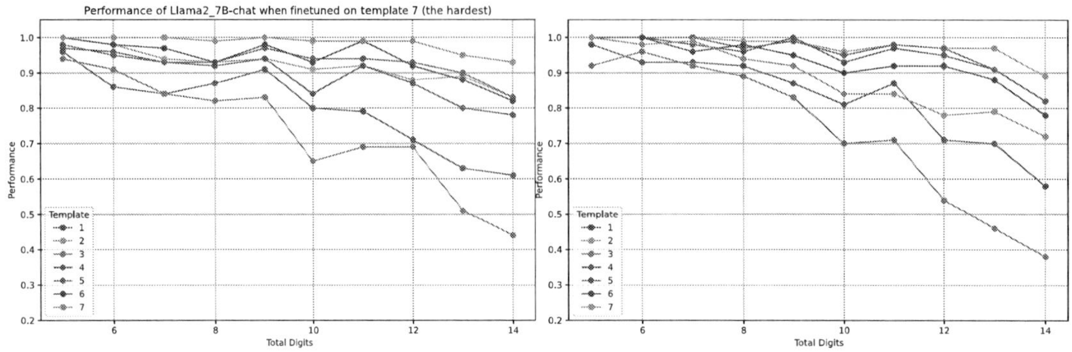

Figure 5: Performance of Llama2 7B chat model when fine-tuned. Left: fine-tuned on the most difficult template #7 (based on the model performance before fine-tuning). Right: fine-tuned on the easiest template #2.

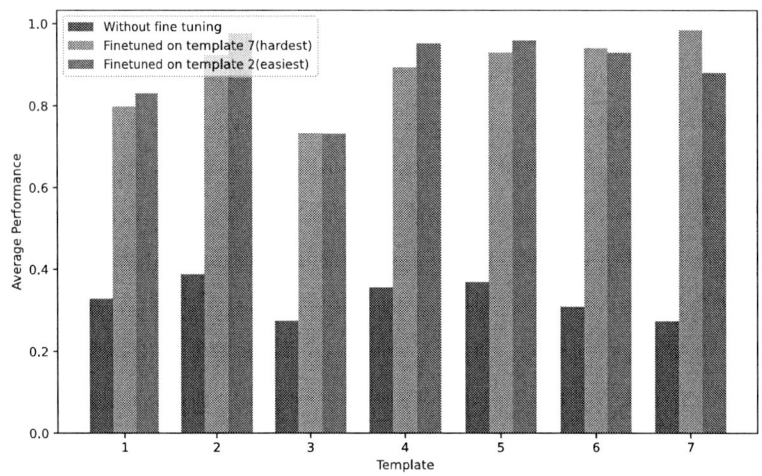

Figure 6: Average performance of Llama2 7B models before and after fine-tuning on templates #2 and #7.

on the most difficult and on the easiest template and measure their performance of the fine-tuned models on all templates variations. As can be seen in Figure 1, for the Llama2 7B chat model, template 2 is the easiest, as on average the performance for this template is higher than those of the others. Template 7 on the other hand, is the most difficult for this model (before fine-tuning).

Figure 5 shows the performance of the fine-tuned models. It is noticeable that performance of the fine-tuned model on templates that have not been used in fine-tuning is affected differently when fine-tuned on templates 2 or 7. Humans are not highly sensitive to the way a question is formulated and in those cases that they are, it is expected that if they learn the hardest rephrased form of a task, they can easily cover the easier variations too. Figure 6 shows that this does not hold for LLMs. Fine-tuning on the easiest template shows better performance on 3 other templates (templates 1, 3, 4 and 5) however, for the case which we fine-tuning on the hardest template the resulting model performs better only on one other template (number 6).

4.2 Diversity of the Contaminating Template

A training set that contains one rephrased item from the test set that is repeated k times has been contaminated in a different way compared to a training set that has k variations of a test item. In the latter case, the diversity of the contaminating template is higher. But does higher diversity cause higher contamination effect in term of performance boost? In order to find out the response to this question, we fine-tuned Llama2 7B model in two different scenarios. In the first scenario, we fine-tune the

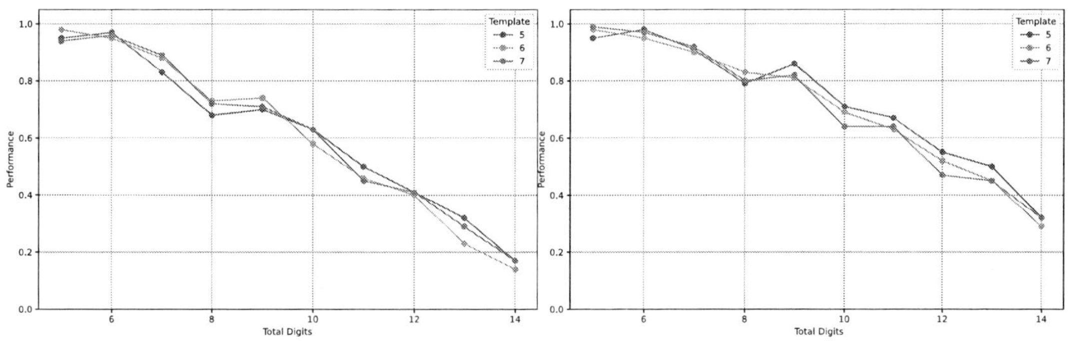

Figure 7: On the left the performance of Llama2 7B chat when fine-tuned one epoch on templates 1, 2, 3 and 4. On the right, performance of the model when fine tuned on a random template between 1, 2, 3 or 4 for four epochs.

model on all instances of templates 1, 2, 3 and 4 and then tested on the remaining templates (5, 6 and 7). The result can be seen in Figure 7 left. In the second scenario, while we use the same test set, the training set contains one random template between 1, 2, 3 and 4 that is repeated 4 times (Figure 7 right). A close look at these figures reveals that if we fix the number of times a rephrased form of a test instance is found in the training set, less diversity has a higher contaminating effect. In our experiments the average performance of the model fine.tuned on diverse templates is 61.4 while we get 71.0 for the less diverse counterpart. This could be due to the fact that in the diverse cases, the model's weights are updated to learn the template and the task which in our case id the addition, but in a less diverse scenario, the model can concentrate on the task as the template wrapping the main task is not changing.

5 Conclusions

Our study explored the effects of data contamination and instance variation on the performance of large language models (LLMs), specifically using fine-tuned LLAMA-2 models on an addition task. Key findings from this investigation answered our research questions and highlighted important insights.

Regarding template difficulty (**RQ1**), we show that the performance of LLMs is significantly influenced by the template or rephrasing of test items. Easier templates, such as Template 2, consistently yielded higher performance, while more complex templates, like Template 7, posed greater challenges. When analysing the impact of fine-tuning on contaminated data (**RQ2**), we observed that performance on non-contaminated templates varies after fine-tuning. Contrary to expectations, some templates showed higher performance on non-contaminated validation sets compared to contaminated test sets, indicating that contamination and difficulty levels are deeply intertwined. Finally, focusing on template diversity and contamination (**RQ3**), we saw that fine-tuning on an easier templates improved performance on other templates more consistently than fine-tuning on harder templates. This challenges the assumption that learning from more difficult examples would generalize better to simpler variations. Additionally, lower template diversity in the training set amplified the contamination effect, suggesting that less diverse contamination scenarios have a stronger influence on model performance.

These findings highlight the relevance of considering both the difficulty and diversity of rephrased instances when evaluating LLM performance. In particular, the change of rephrasing and exemplars can have confounding effects masking contamination or suggesting contamination where there is not. Our results suggest that addressing data contamination effectively requires more nuanced strategies that accommodate these factors. For future work, we are investigating the effects of contamination and instance variation across more complex and diverse NLP tasks.

6 Acknowledgments

We thank the anonymous reviewers for their comments.

This work was funded by ValGRAI, the Norwegian Research Council grant 329745 Machine Teaching for Explainable AI, CIPROM/2022/6 (FASSLOW) and IDIFEDER/2021/05 (CLUSTERIA) funded by Generalitat Valenciana, the EC H2020-EU grant agreement No. 952215 (TAILOR), US DARPA HR00112120007 (RECoG-AI) and Spanish grant PID2021-122830OB-C42 (SFERA) funded by MCIN/AEI/10.13039/501100011033 and "ERDF A way of making Europe".

In compliance with the recommendations of the Science paper about reporting of evaluation results in AI (Burnell et al., 2023), we include all the results at the instance level (`https://github.com/Behzadmeh/ACL-CONDA-2024`).

References

Josh Achiam, Steven Adler, Sandhini Agarwal, Lama Ahmad, Ilge Akkaya, Florencia Leoni Aleman, Diogo Almeida, Janko Altenschmidt, Sam Altman, Shyamal Anadkat, et al. 2023. Gpt-4 technical report. *arXiv preprint arXiv:2303.08774*.

Simone Balloccu, Patrícia Schmidtová, Mateusz Lango, and Ondřej Dušek. 2024. Leak, cheat, repeat: Data contamination and evaluation malpractices in closed-source llms. *arXiv preprint arXiv:2402.03927*.

Tom Brown, Benjamin Mann, Nick Ryder, Melanie Subbiah, Jared D Kaplan, Prafulla Dhariwal, Arvind Neelakantan, Pranav Shyam, Girish Sastry, Amanda Askell, et al. 2020. Language models are few-shot learners. *Advances in neural information processing systems*, 33:1877–1901.

Ryan Burnell, Wout Schellaert, John Burden, Tomer D Ullman, Fernando Martinez-Plumed, Joshua B Tenenbaum, Danaja Rutar, Lucy G Cheke, Jascha Sohl-Dickstein, Melanie Mitchell, Douwe Kiela, Murray Shanahan, Ellen M. Voorhees, Anthony G. Cohn, Joel Z Leibo, and Jose Hernandez-Orallo. 2023. Rethink reporting of evaluation results in AI. *Science*, 380(6641):136–138.

Tim Dettmers, Artidoro Pagnoni, Ari Holtzman, and Luke Zettlemoyer. 2024. Qlora: Efficient finetuning of quantized llms. *Advances in Neural Information Processing Systems*, 36.

Suriya Gunasekar, Yi Zhang, Jyoti Aneja, Caio César Teodoro Mendes, Allie Del Giorno, Sivakanth Gopi, Mojan Javaheripi, Piero Kauffmann, Gustavo de Rosa, Olli Saarikivi, et al. 2023. Textbooks are all you need. *arXiv preprint arXiv:2306.11644*.

Naman Jain, King Han, Alex Gu, Wen-Ding Li, Fanjia Yan, Tianjun Zhang, Sida Wang, Armando Solar-Lezama, Koushik Sen, and Ion Stoica. 2024. Livecodebench: Holistic and contamination free evaluation of large language models for code. *arXiv preprint arXiv:2403.07974*.

Yucheng Li. 2023. An open source data contamination report for llama series models. *arXiv preprint arXiv:2310.17589*.

Alec Radford, Jeffrey Wu, Rewon Child, David Luan, Dario Amodei, Ilya Sutskever, et al. 2019. Language models are unsupervised multitask learners. *OpenAI blog*, 1(8):9.

Federico Ranaldi, Elena Sofia Ruzzetti, Dario Onorati, Leonardo Ranaldi, Cristina Giannone, Andrea Favalli, Raniero Romagnoli, and Fabio Massimo Zanzotto. 2024. Investigating the impact of data contamination of large language models in text-to-sql translation. *arXiv preprint arXiv:2402.08100*.

Mathieu Ravaut, Bosheng Ding, Fangkai Jiao, Hailin Chen, Xingxuan Li, Ruochen Zhao, Chengwei Qin, Caiming Xiong, and Shafiq R. Joty. 2024. How much are llms contaminated? a comprehensive survey and the llmsanitize library. *ArXiv*, abs/2404.00699.

Martin Riddell, Ansong Ni, and Arman Cohan. 2024. Quantifying contamination in evaluating code generation capabilities of language models. *arXiv preprint arXiv:2403.04811*.

Oscar Sainz, Jon Ander Campos, Iker García-Ferrero, Julen Etxaniz, Oier Lopez de Lacalle, and Eneko Agirre. 2023. Nlp evaluation in trouble: On the need to measure llm data contamination for each benchmark. *arXiv preprint arXiv:2310.18018*.

Weijia Shi, Anirudh Ajith, Mengzhou Xia, Yangsibo Huang, Daogao Liu, Terra Blevins, Danqi Chen, and Luke Zettlemoyer. 2023. Detecting pretraining data from large language models. *arXiv preprint arXiv:2310.16789*.

Hugo Touvron, Louis Martin, Kevin Stone, Peter Albert, Amjad Almahairi, Yasmine Babaei, Nikolay Bashlykov, Soumya Batra, Prajjwal Bhargava, Shruti Bhosale, et al. 2023. Llama 2: Open foundation and fine-tuned chat models. *arXiv preprint arXiv:2307.09288*.

Shuo Yang, Wei-Lin Chiang, Lianmin Zheng, Joseph E Gonzalez, and Ion Stoica. 2023. Rethinking benchmark and contamination for language models with rephrased samples. *arXiv preprint arXiv:2311.04850*.

Zhuohao Yu, Chang Gao, Wenjin Yao, Yidong Wang, Wei Ye, Jindong Wang, Xing Xie, Yue Zhang, and Shikun Zhang. 2024. Kieval: A knowledge-grounded interactive evaluation framework for large language models. *arXiv preprint arXiv:2402.15043*.

Wenhong Zhu, Hongkun Hao, Zhiwei He, Yunze Song, Yumeng Zhang, Hanxu Hu, Yiran Wei, Rui Wang, and Hongyuan Lu. 2023. Clean-eval: Clean evaluation on contaminated large language models. *arXiv preprint arXiv:2311.09154*.

A Taxonomy for Data Contamination in Large Language Models

Medha Palavalli and **Amanda Bertsch** and **Matthew R. Gormley**
School of Computer Science
Carnegie Mellon University
[mpalaval, abertsch, mgormley]@cs.cmu.edu

Abstract

Large language models pretrained on extensive web corpora demonstrate remarkable performance across a wide range of downstream tasks. However, a growing concern is data contamination, where evaluation datasets may be contained in the pretraining corpus, inflating model performance. Decontamination, the process of detecting and removing such data, is a potential solution; yet these contaminants may originate from altered versions of the test set, evading detection during decontamination. How different types of contamination impact the performance of language models on downstream tasks is not fully understood. We present a taxonomy that categorizes the various types of contamination encountered by LLMs during the pretraining phase and identify which types pose the highest risk. We analyze the impact of contamination on two key NLP tasks—summarization and question answering—revealing how different types of contamination influence task performance during evaluation.

1 Introduction

Advancements in machine learning have traditionally relied on benchmark datasets to evaluate and compare model performance (Raji et al., 2021; Gururaja et al., 2023). With the surge of large language models (LLMs) in recent years, these benchmarks are now leveraged to showcase remarkable abilities across diverse tasks.

However, the shelf life of benchmarks is incredibly low, with Roberts et al. (2023) demonstrating that newer models with updated training cutoff dates are iteratively rendering existing benchmarks stale. The presence of internet-sourced data in both pretraining and evaluation datasets increases the risk of data contamination (Brown et al., 2020; Magar and Schwartz, 2022) and challenges the notion of fair evaluation for models pretrained on massive corpora. Both GPT-3 and C4 training corpora were found to contain test data for several benchmarks (Dodge et al., 2021; Raffel et al., 2020; Brown et al., 2020), raising serious concerns about the validity of evaluation scores for many pretrained models (Lee et al., 2022; Chang et al., 2023b).

The research community lacks consensus on best practices for data contamination, and different works define contamination in subtly different ways. Without standardization of terminology, it is difficult to develop best practices for contamination– or even to characterize the problem at all. To address this gap, we suggest a formal definition of contamination and taxonomize subtypes of contamination (§ 2). We map prior work on both the detection and impact of contamination into this taxonomy, revealing several understudied forms of contamination (§ 2.3). We also measure the impact of different types of contamination on downstream summarization (§ 4) and QA (§ 5) performance through continued pretraining experiments assessing indirect/approximate test set contamination effects.

Our findings reveal that for GPT-2 Large models, it is often the case that having in-domain data present during training is as beneficial as having the test data present during training. Moreover, we observe that certain contamination types exhibit task-dependent effects on evaluation performance, further complicating decontamination best practices. Our findings enable recommendations for identifying and mitigating problematic contamination during LLM development to ensure reliable evaluations (§ 7).

2 Taxonomy

Consider a model $M : \mathcal{X} \rightarrow \mathcal{Y}$ which, given an input of some type $x \in \mathcal{X}$, outputs text $\widehat{y} \in \mathcal{Y}$. While x can be of any format, we will restrict ourselves to cases where $\widehat{y}$ is in the space of the *natural language* ($\mathcal{Y} \subseteq \Sigma^*$ for some alphabet in Σ). Let D be the *test* set, consisting of $|D|$ examples $\langle x_i, \widehat{y}_i \rangle$.

Proceedings of the 1st Workshop on Data Contamination (CONDA), pages 22–40
August 16, 2024

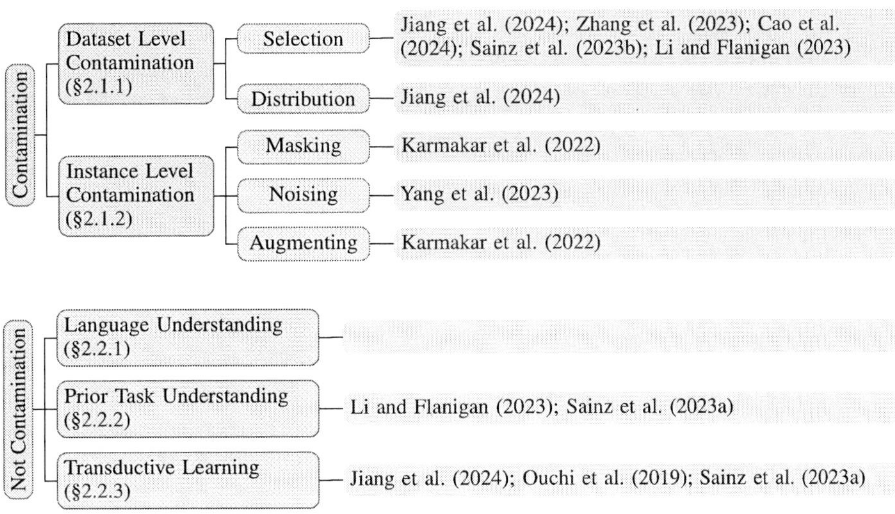

Figure 1: Taxonomy of Contamination, with some representative works in the literature that address each category.

2.1 Contamination

We define **contamination** as any leakage of information that provides a signal for the correct label for at least one example in the test set D. When contamination occurs, some subset of the pretraining data can be characterized as the result of a function $f(D)$, which may be a composition of multiple contamination functions $f = f^{(1)} \circ f^{(2)} \circ \cdots \circ f^{(n)}$. We characterize types of contamination by their *dataset-level* (§ 2.1.1) and *example-level* (§ 2.1.2) properties. Figure 1 provides an overview of our taxonomy.

2.1.1 Dataset-level Properties

For dataset-level contamination, consider a function g that leaves the individual examples $\langle x_i, \widehat{y}_i \rangle$ intact. In the simplest case, g is the identity function; this is the leakage of a full test set, e.g. from scraping a file containing the test set instances and labels. The following are types of functions $g(D)$ can take on.

- **Selection:** A function that selects some group of examples $D' \subset D$, such that only a subset of the test set is leaked. This is likely when the test data is drawn from several sources, only some of which appear in the pretraining data; when some of the test data is more recent than other data and the pretraining data contains an older snapshot of the contamination source; or when the data is contained in several documents and the cleaning of the pretraining data only removes some of these documents. *Verbatim contamination* refers to when g is the identity function.
- **Distribution:** A function which combines the contaminated data D with some additional, non-contaminating documents, such that the examples from D are not all sequential in the pretraining data. This can occur during data shuffling, or if the contamination comes from multiple documents. Practically, this means that the contaminated region of the pretraining data $g(D)$ spans more tokens.

2.1.2 Instance-level Properties

In instance-level contamination, the function f applies some function h to each individual leaked example $f(D) = \{h(\langle x_i, \widehat{y}_i \rangle)\}_{i=1}^{|D|}$.[1] A few representative examples in this class are enumerated below:

- **Masking:** A function that removes some or all of the input (can be done in combination with the output), e.g. $h(\langle x_i, \widehat{y}_i \rangle) = \widehat{y}_i$ or removing all incorrect answer choices in a multiple choice question. *This primarily qualifies as contamination for generation tasks;* for a classification task, leaking the label-space in advance may not be a concern if the labels don't have inherent contextual value without the input, such as binary labels like 0s and 1s or positives and negatives. However, if the

[1]Note that this is a strict subset of all functions applied to the leaked dataset, $f(D)$; however, we distinguish this set of functions that operate on individual examples.

labels carry meaningful information on their own, their premature disclosure would indeed constitute contamination. Note that masking *all of the output*, leaving only the inputs from the test set, is generally considered to be a type of transductive learning, *not* contamination; see § 2.2.3 for more discussion.

- **Noising:** A function that modifies the surface form of the example, e.g. by paraphrasing the inputs or outputs, by presenting the output before the input, or by using silver rather than gold labels for each example. Note that this can also take the form of *alternate correct answers* being present in the pretraining data: for instance, in book summarization, a different summary of the book being present in the pretraining data is still contamination.

- **Augmenting:** A function that adds additional context, which may or may not be relevant to the example. For instance, for a task where the model must answer an open-ended question at test time, an *augmented* contaminated example in pretraining would be a multiple-choice test with the same questions. While this provides the correct answer, it also introduces new (distractor) information that is not present at test time. Another example would be including additional context paragraphs for QA in addition to the necessary context and answer. Note the difference between example-level *augmenting* and dataset-level *distribution*.

2.2 Phenomena that aren't Contamination

For clarity, we describe several phenomena that lead to improved performance on test sets downstream but are *not* considered contamination under our taxonomy.

2.2.1 Language Understanding

Pretraining enables models to produce (generally) fluent text and encodes some representation of meaning for words commonly used in task definitions; for instance, the model has some representation of meaning for the labels "positive" and "negative" in sentiment analysis. While this representation is likely helpful for performing downstream tasks (Min et al., 2022), this is not inherently contamination.

2.2.2 Prior Task Understanding

We define prior task understanding as an ability to perform a task learned from non-contamination sources, and such prior knowledge has been demonstrated to boost model performance when evaluated on unseen instances of said task (Li and Flanigan, 2023). For instance, fine-tuning a model on a training dataset for the task is clearly not contamination of the test set, although it generally improves performance on that test set; likewise, pretraining on other related datasets is not contamination for a given test set. For closed-book QA and tasks requiring world knowledge, prior task understanding from training data is essential. Closed-book QA demands answering without external resources, relying solely on the model's training on similar question-answer pairs or related datasets.

In general, scrutinizing the training data's sources and nature is crucial to maintain model integrity and generalizability. Prior task understanding may violate the assumption of "zero-shot" performance: that the model has not seen training data for that task.

2.2.3 Transductive Learning

Transductive learning (Vapnik, 1998) incorporates an unlabeled test set into training. During training, the raw text inputs of the test set can be used, but the labels are not seen. The model, once trained, is then evaluated on the same test set during the test phase. Transductive LM fine-tuning has shown to consistently improve neural models in both in-domain and out-of-domain settings (Ouchi et al., 2019), although concerns have been raised about blurring the line between training and evaluation (Jiang et al., 2024).

We generally do not consider pretraining on the *inputs* of the test set to be contamination,[2] although we note that this will likely improve performance, in the same manner than pretraining on training set text improves downstream performance by providing some domain adaptation to the testing domain (Gururangan et al., 2020; Krishna et al., 2023). Some prior work refers to the presence of inputs-only in the pretraining data as contamination for classification tasks (Jiang et al., 2024; Ouchi et al., 2019); however, under our taxonomy, we consider this a type of transductive learning.

[2]A key exception is tasks where the input/output distinction does not apply, such as perplexity evaluation on a dataset $D = \{x_1, \ldots, x_{|D|}\}$ of sentences x_i.

2.3 Mapping prior work exploring contamination into this taxonomy

The effects of *selection* have been explored by experiments that compare LLM performance over time (Li and Flanigan, 2023; Cao et al., 2024), prompting the model to generate samples from specific dataset splits (Sainz et al., 2023b), and training LLMs that *select* some subset of an evaluation dataset (Zhang et al., 2023; Jiang et al., 2024).

Jiang et al. (2024) also explores the effects of the frequency in which contaminated data appears *distributed* throughout the pretraining data.

Through zero-shot experimentation on the Codex model (Chen et al., 2021), Karmakar et al. (2022) investigates the effects of prompts *masking* out input specifications and prompts with *augmented* objectives. Additionally, Yang et al. (2023) showcases memorization of evaluation samples by prompting LLMs with *noisy* samples.

A prior position paper (Sainz et al., 2023a) defined three categories of data contamination: their *guideline contamination* falls under our definition of prior task understanding; their *raw text contamination* is tranductive learning; and their *annotation contamination* equates to our definition of data contamination in § 2.1. Our work further categorizes and explores types of annotation contamination.

2.4 Detecting Data Contamination

Methods with access to pretraining data Early research on LLM data contamination primarily employed methods akin to high-order n-gram overlap detection between pretraining and evaluation data (Radford et al., 2019a; Brown et al., 2020; Wei et al., 2021; Touvron et al., 2023). Tools for qualitative analysis on large-scale corpora (such as Data Portraits (Marone and Durme, 2023) and the ROOTS Search Tool (Piktus et al., 2023)) have further increased the practicality of this type of contamination detection. However, these approaches have several limitations: they remain fairly computationally expensive, assume access to pretraining data, and generally can only detect contamination when a cluster of several test set examples co-occur (as most methods leverage data sketching (Broder, 1997) tools that are only effective for sequences above a certain length).

Yang et al. (2023) proposes an LLM-based decontamination method, which leverages embedding similarity search followed by evaluation with a strong language model (e.g. GPT-4), to identify and mitigate contamination. This is computationally costly but can identify *noisy* contamination

Methods without access to pretraining data Some approaches are capable of detecting contamination without direct access to pretraining data, but assume that the test data has not been modified or distributed across the pretraining corpus. These methods leverage *metadata* from the dataset to detect contamination, e.g. by leveraging dataset ordering (Sainz et al., 2023b) or the assignment of examples to specific data splits (Golchin and Surdeanu, 2023). Golchin and Surdeanu (2024) introduce the Data Contamination Quiz, a streamlined method that efficiently detects and estimates verbatim contamination in LLMs by crafting multiple choice questions that prompt a model to correctly dataset-specific content among similar but noisy alternatives.

Chang et al. (2023a) detect contamination of books (which serve as inputs for many long-context evaluation datasets) using domain specific features– a name cloze test and a publication-year evaluation. This is powerful for detecting the presence of the exact text of the book, but its efficacy on detecting related artifacts (e.g. summaries of the book, which may serve as test set outputs) is unknown.

Shi et al. (2023) introduces a new detection method MIN-K% PROB, which is capable of detecting whether a piece of text was in the pretraining corpora by leveraging the variability of the tokens' probabilities according to the model. This has the potential to detect distributed or masked contamination, but is not robust to noising operations, which change the token sequence.

Most contemporary data-contamination detection techniques are designed to identify contamination of full, non-distributed test datasets, resulting in a significant gap in detecting noisy or partial contamination. The methods most well-adapted to detect noisy contamination, while powerful, require access to pretraining data and expensive operations; more work is necessary to lower the barrier to detection.

3 Methodology

In all our experiments, we employ GPT-2 Large (Radford et al., 2019b).[3] This will be referred to as the *initial model*. Since the pretraining corpus for GPT-2 is not publicly accessible, there is a chance

[3] Our implementation uses nanoGPT (Karpathy, 2023) initialized with OpenAI's `gpt2-large` weights.

that these *learned* weights of GPT-2 might be contaminated. Consequently, the outcomes of our experiments serve as a conservative estimate or lower bound on the effects of data contamination.

For each of our datasets, we create `train/in-domain/test` splits of equal size, aiming to establish a fair and comparable evaluation environment. To disentangle the effects of exposure to `test` data during pretraining from those of prior task understanding, we constructed an `in-domain` data split, allowing us to train models on task-relevant but uncontaminated data for comparison against the various contaminated settings. To partially mitigate the potential recency bias from continued pretraining, we incorporate an additional 10,000 samples of Open AI's WebText (Radford et al., 2019b) into the continued pretraining data.

During continued pretraining, we use a blocksize of 1024 tokens with a batchsize of 1. For finetuning, the training data is seen sample by sample. To obtain deterministic results during our experiments, we set the temperature to zero and capped the maximum completion length at 200 tokens.

3.1 Training Settings

We consider several settings for incorporating data:

- ZERO-SHOT (not contamination): prompt the initial model with the test sample and a simple instruction for the task.
- BASELINE (not contamination): finetune initial model with `train` split
- CHEATING (contamination at fine-tuning time, rather than pre-training): finetune initial model with `test` split
- *Contamination Setting(s)* (standard contamination during pretraining): continued pretraining with $f($`test` split) and finetune with `train` split; the details of each contamination setting are specific to the task (§ 4 and § 5)
- *In-Domain Setting(s)* (not contamination): continued pretraining with $f($`in-domain` split) and finetune with `train` split—for each contamination setting in § 4 and § 5, there is an associated in-domain model.

For each setting+dataset, we average results over models trained on 3 random shuffles of the data. Standard deviations are computed over these 3 runs and error bars indicate $\pm$ one standard deviation.

4 Case Study: Summarization

For this case study, we use the following summarization datasets: XSum (Narayan et al., 2018), SAMSum (Gliwa et al., 2019), and CNN/Daily Mail (Nallapati et al., 2016). We explore 5 contamination settings:

1. VERBATIM (dataset level, selection): $f =$ identity function on `test` split
2. DISTRIBUTION (dataset level, distribution): $f =$ shuffle `test` data with WebText
3. MASKED (instance level, masking): $h =$ mask out input documents in `test` split
4. NOISED (instance level, noising): $h =$ swap in GPT-3.5[4] generated summaries on `test` split
5. REFORMATTED (instance level, noising): $h =$ swap format from document-summary to summary-document for `test` data

Table 5 provides examples of each setting.

4.1 Results

In this section, we consider the overall performance of each contamination method across summarization datasets. Figure 2 shows an example of the results from one task and one metric (SAMSum, ROUGE-L). See Appendix A for full results on all tasks and metrics, specifically Figures 4, 5, 6 or Table 3.

Consistently, the CHEATING setting outperforms all others; this is expected, given that deliberately finetuning on the `test` data is an extreme form of contamination.

Overall, continued pretraining with the approximate contamination methods improves performance above the BASELINE setting, often substantially. This suggests that exposure to these forms of contamination during pretraining can impact the reliability of evaluations on this data downstream.

While VERBATIM setting performs slightly better than the other contamination settings, this improvement isn't significant for most settings. Note that most contaminated settings outperform the baseline, and exist within a standard deviation of each other. This suggests that the performance boost may simply be attributed to the increase in `in-domain` data seen during the training stage rather than encountering the `test` split during continued pretraining.

Note that for the most part, the VERBATIM and INDOMAIN-VERBATIM settings perform on par

[4] `gpt-3.5-turbo-0125` with temperature=0.5

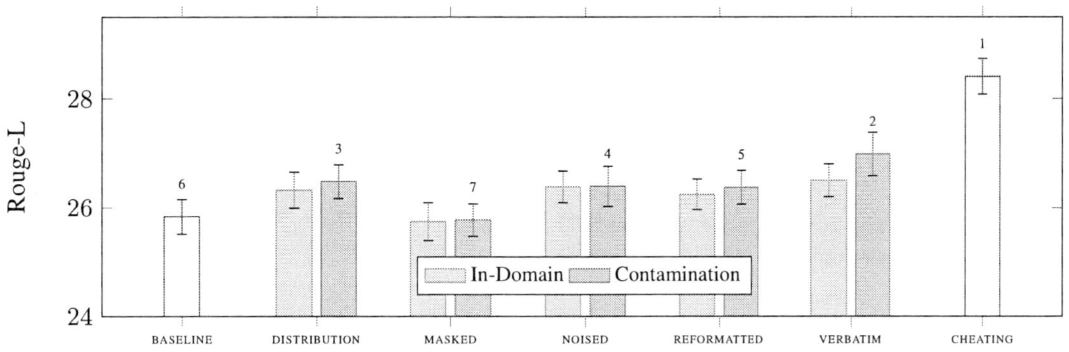

Figure 2: Bar Chart of all SAMSum models compared for Rouge-L.

with each other. This trend seems to hold true for the other *contamination* and *in-domain* model pairs. The comparable performance further suggests that exposure to contaminated data may not be the primary factor boosting model performance in the *contamination* settings studied.

Dataset	R-1	R-2	R-L	R-Lsum
CNN	38.70	14.14	24.90	32.11
SAMSum	37.92	13.78	28.73	28.75
XSum	24.21	4.89	16.60	16.60

Table 1: Rouge scores (R-) for summaries generated by GPT-3.5. These summaries are used as silver labels for our NOISED contamination setting.

While the majority of these settings have metrics that fall within one standard deviation of each other, there are exceptions. For instance, in the case of the XSum dataset, the NOISED setting fails to surpass the BASELINE. This discrepancy can be attributed to the idiosyncrasies of the XSum dataset, where ground truth summaries may deviate significantly from typical summaries, thus posing a challenge for the model in generating accurate outputs. Table 1 shows that the summaries generated by GPT-3.5 (Brown et al., 2020) for the XSum dataset have lower rouge scores than the other two datasets.

Additionally, underperformance of the MASKED contamination setting compared to the BASELINE across all datasets is noteworthy, suggesting that exposure only to summaries during pretraining may fail to achieve the benefits of seeing `in-domain` data.

5 Case Study: Question Answering

For this case study, we consider open-ended QA with SQuAD (Rajpurkar et al., 2016) and multiple-choice QA with the Children's Book Test (CBT) (Hill et al., 2016). We explore 6 contamination settings:

1. VERBATIM (dataset level, selection): f = identity function on `test` split
2. DISTRIBUTION (dataset level, distribution): f = shuffle `test data` with WebText
3. MASKED (instance level, masking): h = mask out context passage in `test` split
4. NOISED (instance level, noising): h = encounter GPT-3.5 generated answers to `test split` questions
5. REFORMATTED (instance level, augmenting/-masking)[5]: h_{SQuAD} = introduce 3 distractor multiple choice answer options; h_{CBT} = mask out incorrect answer options
6. AUGMENTED (instance level, augmenting): h = prompt GPT-3.5 to add additional content to the context passages in the `test` split

Table 6 provides examples of each setting.

5.1 Results

In this section, we consider the overall performance of each contamination method across Question Answering datasets. Figure 3 shows an example of the results from one task and one metric (SQuAD, Exact Match). See Appendix B for full evaluation results on all tasks and metrics, specifically Figures 7, 8 or Table 4.

Once again, the CHEATING setting outperforms all others by a noticeable margin. With the exception of the MASKED setting for the SQuAD

[5]For SQuAD, this is a form of augmented contamination, as additional (distractor) information is introduced. For CBT, this is a form of masked contamination, as information is removed.

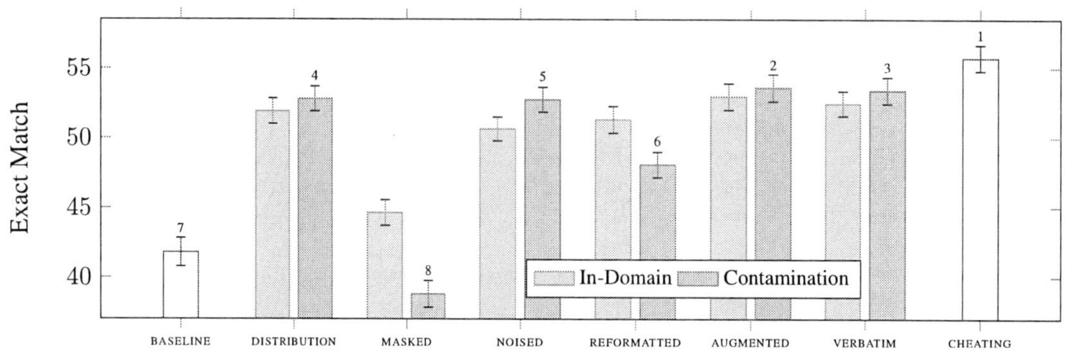

Figure 3: Bar Chart of all SQuAD models compared for Exact Match.

dataset, all contaminated settings exhibit better performance compared to the BASELINE setting by a considerable margin. This indicates that the increased data diversity experienced by both the *in-domain* and *contaminated* models during training improved their performance during evaluation.

Dataset	Exact Match	F1 Score
SQuAD	74.56	88.15
CBT	77.21	79.78

Table 2: Exact match and F1 scores for answers generated by GPT-3.5.

Note that the NOISED setting performs almost as well as the VERBATIM contamination setting. We attribute this to the fairly high quality of silver labels generated by GPT-3.5 (see Table 2).

Exposure to `in-domain` data during pretraining appears to improve model performance. However, our results show that contaminated settings such as NOISED, VERBATIM, and DISTRIBUTION tend to outperform the corresponding *in-domain* settings during evaluation. This suggests that seeing data from the `test` set positively impacts model performance for question answering tasks. Note that for these three model setups, the format of context, question, and answer is almost consistent with the format and content seen during evaluation time.

Reformatting (augmenting) free-form questions from SQuAD into multiple-choice answers during pretraining appears to have a negative effect on model performance, though it still outperforms the BASELINE setting. Conversely, converting multiple-choice questions from CBT into free-form questions (masking) during pretraining yields positive results, with the REFORMATTED setting outperforming most other contaminated settings.

Furthermore, we observe variations in the performance of AUGMENTED setting across the two datasets. While this setting perform well for SQuAD, its performance is not as impressive for CBT. This discrepancy may be attributed to the nature of data augmentation, where the additional information provided for SQuAD is more relevant and beneficial to the wikipedia paragraphs compared to the irrelevant introductions, such as 'once upon a time' style introductions generated by GPT-3.5 for these book excerpts, added to CBT stories. It is important to note that since this information doesn't significantly contribute to the task, this form of augmentation falls in a blurry space between distribution and augmentation branches of the taxonomy. It could also be viewed as unrelated information being added between samples during pretraining, complicating its categorization.

6 Analysis

Unsurprisingly, the CHEATING and VERBATIM contamination settings consistently outperform the BASELINE across both tasks. The *in-domain* settings' consistent outperformance of the BASELINE underscores the advantages of exposure to related samples during pretraining (Krishna et al., 2023).

Far more concerning is that several approximate contamination settings outperform both the BASELINE and their respective *in-domain* settings, suggesting that the model in these settings benefits not only from seeing in-domain text but from unfairly leveraging prior knowledge of the test examples. In particular, the NOISED setting, which is generally not detectable with existing decontamination methods, produces scores inflated over BASELINE in all datasets, and scores more than one standard deviation above its corresponding *in-domain* setting in several datasets.

The MASKED setting generally performs around or worse than the BASELINE, possibly due to the more extreme formatting mismatch between this data and the test data. We expect that the MASKED setting may be encountered in the wild if a file of outputs for the dataset is in the pretraining data; the limited impact of this contamination on downstream performance is thus good news, though more investigation would be necessary to conclusively say MASKED contamination is not a concern.

For many of the *contaminated* settings and their corresponding *in-domain* settings, the effect of approximate contamination is not greater than affect of `in-domain` data seen during pretaining. However, research has shown that memorization in LLMs significantly grows as the size of the model increases (Carlini et al., 2023). The number of times a sample has been duplicated in the pretraining corpora has also been shown to increase a model's memorization capabilities (Carlini et al., 2023; Golchin and Surdeanu, 2023).

Some behavior is task- or dataset-specific, emphasizing that there is no one-size-fits-all approach to data curation: the importance of removing each type of contamination from the pretraining corpus is at least partially linked to the specific task's formatting. However, some types of approximate contamination do lead to inflated scores, emphasizing that considering a more broad definition of contamination when de-contaminating pretraining corpora is a worthwhile endeavor.

7 Conclusion

Our analysis highlights the importance of data format, with models performing better when pretraining data matches the evaluation format. We also observe task-specific effects, with certain contamination methods benefiting particular tasks more than others. Additionally, we find that some late-stage pretraining contamination can actually be *unhelpful* to downstream performance, if it occurs in a substantially different format from the downstream task. Our findings underscore gaps in current decontamination practices, which primarily focus on full-dataset-level contamination and are often unable to detect approximate or noisy contamination.

We demonstrate that different types of contamination can have variable effects on model performance, highlighting the need for careful consideration during training and evaluation. With the creation of our taxonomy, we hope to promote standardization regarding the definition and categories of contamination within the research community, facilitating clear communication and collaboration, while also enabling precise detection and mitigation of contamination in pretraining data. We recommend researchers decontaminating pretraining corpora for LLMs prioritize developing techniques that address noisy evaluation data, while also ensuring rigorous scrutiny to prevent any shuffled or interleaved evaluation data from inadvertently persisting in the pretraining data. It is not enough to merely remove instances of the full test dataset in the pretraining corpus; fragments or noised versions of the test set can also inflate performance. We hope our work inspires future work on detecting and mitigating specific types of contamination.

8 Limitations

Due to resource constraints, we only investigate the impact of encountering contaminated data towards the end of pretraining (i.e. with continued pretraining), rather than randomly throughout pretraining. This may introduce recency bias, influencing our findings. Additionally, our focus on a single language model limits the generalizability of our results. GPT-2 pretraining data is not publicly accessible so our results may only offer an approximation of contamination effects. Different model architectures, training procedures, and datasets may yield varying impacts of contamination. Conducting experiments on larger LLMs could potentially reveal more pronounced effects of contamination, as larger models have been shown to exhibit greater tendencies of memorization (Carlini et al., 2023). Further research involving multiple models and comprehensive evaluations is needed to establish more robust conclusions across diverse settings.

Acknowledgements

The authors would like to thank Lori Levin for her early guidance and the anonymous reviewers for their thoughtful comments. This work was supported in part by grants from 3M, the Pittsburgh Supercomputing Center, and the National Science Foundation Graduate Research Fellowship under Grant No. DGE2140739.

References

A.Z. Broder. 1997. On the resemblance and containment of documents. In *Proceedings. Compression and Complexity of SEQUENCES 1997 (Cat. No.97TB100171)*, pages 21–29.

Tom B. Brown, Benjamin Mann, Nick Ryder, Melanie Subbiah, Jared Kaplan, Prafulla Dhariwal, Arvind Neelakantan, Pranav Shyam, Girish Sastry, Amanda Askell, Sandhini Agarwal, Ariel Herbert-Voss, Gretchen Krueger, Tom Henighan, Rewon Child, Aditya Ramesh, Daniel M. Ziegler, Jeffrey Wu, Clemens Winter, Christopher Hesse, Mark Chen, Eric Sigler, Mateusz Litwin, Scott Gray, Benjamin Chess, Jack Clark, Christopher Berner, Sam McCandlish, Alec Radford, Ilya Sutskever, and Dario Amodei. 2020. Language models are few-shot learners.

Jialun Cao, Wuqi Zhang, and Shing-Chi Cheung. 2024. Concerned with data contamination? assessing countermeasures in code language model.

Nicholas Carlini, Daphne Ippolito, Matthew Jagielski, Katherine Lee, Florian Tramer, and Chiyuan Zhang. 2023. Quantifying memorization across neural language models.

Kent K. Chang, Mackenzie Cramer, Sandeep Soni, and David Bamman. 2023a. Speak, memory: An archaeology of books known to chatgpt/gpt-4.

Yupeng Chang, Xu Wang, Jindong Wang, Yuan Wu, Linyi Yang, Kaijie Zhu, Hao Chen, Xiaoyuan Yi, Cunxiang Wang, Yidong Wang, Wei Ye, Yue Zhang, Yi Chang, Philip S. Yu, Qiang Yang, and Xing Xie. 2023b. A survey on evaluation of large language models.

Mark Chen, Jerry Tworek, Heewoo Jun, Qiming Yuan, Henrique Ponde de Oliveira Pinto, Jared Kaplan, Harri Edwards, Yuri Burda, Nicholas Joseph, Greg Brockman, Alex Ray, Raul Puri, Gretchen Krueger, Michael Petrov, Heidy Khlaaf, Girish Sastry, Pamela Mishkin, Brooke Chan, Scott Gray, Nick Ryder, Mikhail Pavlov, Alethea Power, Lukasz Kaiser, Mohammad Bavarian, Clemens Winter, Philippe Tillet, Felipe Petroski Such, Dave Cummings, Matthias Plappert, Fotios Chantzis, Elizabeth Barnes, Ariel Herbert-Voss, William Hebgen Guss, Alex Nichol, Alex Paino, Nikolas Tezak, Jie Tang, Igor Babuschkin, Suchir Balaji, Shantanu Jain, William Saunders, Christopher Hesse, Andrew N. Carr, Jan Leike, Josh Achiam, Vedant Misra, Evan Morikawa, Alec Radford, Matthew Knight, Miles Brundage, Mira Murati, Katie Mayer, Peter Welinder, Bob McGrew, Dario Amodei, Sam McCandlish, Ilya Sutskever, and Wojciech Zaremba. 2021. Evaluating large language models trained on code.

Jesse Dodge, Maarten Sap, Ana Marasović, William Agnew, Gabriel Ilharco, Dirk Groeneveld, Margaret Mitchell, and Matt Gardner. 2021. Documenting large webtext corpora: A case study on the colossal clean crawled corpus. In *Proceedings of the 2021 Conference on Empirical Methods in Natural Language Processing*, pages 1286–1305, Online and Punta Cana, Dominican Republic. Association for Computational Linguistics.

Bogdan Gliwa, Iwona Mochol, Maciej Biesek, and Aleksander Wawer. 2019. SAMSum corpus: A human-annotated dialogue dataset for abstractive summarization. In *Proceedings of the 2nd Workshop on New Frontiers in Summarization*, pages 70–79, Hong Kong, China. Association for Computational Linguistics.

Shahriar Golchin and Mihai Surdeanu. 2023. Time travel in llms: Tracing data contamination in large language models.

Shahriar Golchin and Mihai Surdeanu. 2024. Data contamination quiz: A tool to detect and estimate contamination in large language models.

Sireesh Gururaja, Amanda Bertsch, Clara Na, David Widder, and Emma Strubell. 2023. To build our future, we must know our past: Contextualizing paradigm shifts in natural language processing. In *Proceedings of the 2023 Conference on Empirical Methods in Natural Language Processing*, pages 13310–13325, Singapore. Association for Computational Linguistics.

Suchin Gururangan, Ana Marasović, Swabha Swayamdipta, Kyle Lo, Iz Beltagy, Doug Downey, and Noah A. Smith. 2020. Don't stop pretraining: Adapt language models to domains and tasks. In *Proceedings of the 58th Annual Meeting of the Association for Computational Linguistics*, pages 8342–8360, Online. Association for Computational Linguistics.

Felix Hill, Antoine Bordes, Sumit Chopra, and Jason Weston. 2016. The goldilocks principle: Reading children's books with explicit memory representations.

Minhao Jiang, Ken Ziyu Liu, Ming Zhong, Rylan Schaeffer, Siru Ouyang, Jiawei Han, and Sanmi Koyejo. 2024. Investigating data contamination for pre-training language models.

Anjan Karmakar, Julian Aron Prenner, Marco D'Ambros, and Romain Robbes. 2022. Codex hacks hackerrank: Memorization issues and a framework for code synthesis evaluation.

Andrej Karpathy. 2023. nanogpt.

Kundan Krishna, Saurabh Garg, Jeffrey P. Bigham, and Zachary C. Lipton. 2023. Downstream datasets make surprisingly good pretraining corpora.

Katherine Lee, Daphne Ippolito, Andrew Nystrom, Chiyuan Zhang, Douglas Eck, Chris Callison-Burch, and Nicholas Carlini. 2022. Deduplicating training data makes language models better. In *Proceedings of the 60th Annual Meeting of the Association for Computational Linguistics (Volume 1: Long Papers)*, pages 8424–8445, Dublin, Ireland. Association for Computational Linguistics.

Changmao Li and Jeffrey Flanigan. 2023. Task contamination: Language models may not be few-shot anymore.

Inbal Magar and Roy Schwartz. 2022. Data contamination: From memorization to exploitation.

Marc Marone and Benjamin Van Durme. 2023. Data portraits: Recording foundation model training data.

Sewon Min, Xinxi Lyu, Ari Holtzman, Mikel Artetxe, Mike Lewis, Hannaneh Hajishirzi, and Luke Zettlemoyer. 2022. Rethinking the role of demonstrations: What makes in-context learning work? In *Proceedings of the 2022 Conference on Empirical Methods in Natural Language Processing*, pages 11048–11064, Abu Dhabi, United Arab Emirates. Association for Computational Linguistics.

Ramesh Nallapati, Bowen Zhou, Cicero dos Santos, Çağlar Gulçehre, and Bing Xiang. 2016. Abstractive text summarization using sequence-to-sequence RNNs and beyond. In *Proceedings of the 20th SIGNLL Conference on Computational Natural Language Learning*, pages 280–290, Berlin, Germany. Association for Computational Linguistics.

Shashi Narayan, Shay B. Cohen, and Mirella Lapata. 2018. Don't give me the details, just the summary! topic-aware convolutional neural networks for extreme summarization. In *Proceedings of the 2018 Conference on Empirical Methods in Natural Language Processing*, pages 1797–1807, Brussels, Belgium. Association for Computational Linguistics.

Hiroki Ouchi, Jun Suzuki, and Kentaro Inui. 2019. Transductive learning of neural language models for syntactic and semantic analysis. In *Proceedings of the 2019 Conference on Empirical Methods in Natural Language Processing and the 9th International Joint Conference on Natural Language Processing (EMNLP-IJCNLP)*, pages 3665–3671, Hong Kong, China. Association for Computational Linguistics.

Aleksandra Piktus, Christopher Akiki, Paulo Villegas, Hugo Laurençon, Gérard Dupont, Alexandra Sasha Luccioni, Yacine Jernite, and Anna Rogers. 2023. The roots search tool: Data transparency for llms.

Alec Radford, Jeffrey Wu, Rewon Child, David Luan, Dario Amodei, and Ilya Sutskever. 2019a. Language models are unsupervised multitask learners.

Alec Radford, Jeffrey Wu, Rewon Child, David Luan, Dario Amodei, Ilya Sutskever, et al. 2019b. Language models are unsupervised multitask learners. *OpenAI blog*, 1(8):9.

Colin Raffel, Noam Shazeer, Adam Roberts, Katherine Lee, Sharan Narang, Michael Matena, Yanqi Zhou, Wei Li, and Peter J. Liu. 2020. Exploring the limits of transfer learning with a unified text-to-text transformer. *CoRR*, abs/1910.10683.

Inioluwa Deborah Raji, Emily M. Bender, Amandalynne Paullada, Emily Denton, and Alex Hanna. 2021. Ai and the everything in the whole wide world benchmark.

Pranav Rajpurkar, Jian Zhang, Konstantin Lopyrev, and Percy Liang. 2016. SQuAD: 100,000+ questions for machine comprehension of text. In *Proceedings of the 2016 Conference on Empirical Methods in Natural Language Processing*, pages 2383–2392, Austin, Texas. Association for Computational Linguistics.

Manley Roberts, Himanshu Thakur, Christine Herlihy, Colin White, and Samuel Dooley. 2023. Data contamination through the lens of time.

Oscar Sainz, Jon Campos, Iker García-Ferrero, Julen Etxaniz, Oier Lopez de Lacalle, and Eneko Agirre. 2023a. NLP evaluation in trouble: On the need to measure LLM data contamination for each benchmark. In *Findings of the Association for Computational Linguistics: EMNLP 2023*, pages 10776–10787, Singapore. Association for Computational Linguistics.

Oscar Sainz, Jon Ander Campos, Iker Garcia-Ferrero, Julen Etxaniz, , and Eneko Agirre. 2023b. Did chatgpt cheat on your test?

Weijia Shi, Anirudh Ajith, Mengzhou Xia, Yangsibo Huang, Daogao Liu, Terra Blevins, Danqi Chen, and Luke Zettlemoyer. 2023. Detecting pretraining data from large language models.

Hugo Touvron, Louis Martin, Kevin Stone, Peter Albert, Amjad Almahairi, Yasmine Babaei, Nikolay Bashlykov, Soumya Batra, Prajjwal Bhargava, Shruti Bhosale, Dan Bikel, Lukas Blecher, Cristian Canton Ferrer, Moya Chen, Guillem Cucurull, David Esiobu, Jude Fernandes, Jeremy Fu, Wenyin Fu, Brian Fuller, Cynthia Gao, Vedanuj Goswami, Naman Goyal, Anthony Hartshorn, Saghar Hosseini, Rui Hou, Hakan Inan, Marcin Kardas, Viktor Kerkez, Madian Khabsa, Isabel Kloumann, Artem Korenev, Punit Singh Koura, Marie-Anne Lachaux, Thibaut Lavril, Jenya Lee, Diana Liskovich, Yinghai Lu, Yuning Mao, Xavier Martinet, Todor Mihaylov, Pushkar Mishra, Igor Molybog, Yixin Nie, Andrew Poulton, Jeremy Reizenstein, Rashi Rungta, Kalyan Saladi, Alan Schelten, Ruan Silva, Eric Michael Smith, Ranjan Subramanian, Xiaoqing Ellen Tan, Binh Tang, Ross Taylor, Adina Williams, Jian Xiang Kuan, Puxin Xu, Zheng Yan, Iliyan Zarov, Yuchen Zhang, Angela Fan, Melanie Kambadur, Sharan Narang, Aurelien Rodriguez, Robert Stojnic, Sergey Edunov, and Thomas Scialom. 2023. Llama 2: Open foundation and fine-tuned chat models.

Vladimir Vapnik. 1998. Statistical learning theory. *John Wiley & Sons*.

Jason Wei, Maarten Bosma, Vincent Y. Zhao, Kelvin Guu, Adams Wei Yu, Brian Lester, Nan Du, Andrew M. Dai, and Quoc V. Le. 2021. Finetuned language models are zero-shot learners. *CoRR*, abs/2109.01652.

Shuo Yang, Wei-Lin Chiang, Lianmin Zheng, Joseph E. Gonzalez, and Ion Stoica. 2023. Rethinking benchmark and contamination for language models with rephrased samples.

Chiyuan Zhang, Daphne Ippolito, Katherine Lee, Matthew Jagielski, Florian Tramèr, and Nicholas Carlini. 2023. Counterfactual memorization in neural language models.

A Full results for Summarization Case Study

We present the full results of the summarization case study. For each setting and dataset, we have included a table of the Rouge metrics along with their standard deviations. The data is also presented through a series of bar charts for easier interpretability of the results for the reader. Standard deviations are measured over the results of the 3 models trained on random shuffles of the data.

Dataset	Model	Contaminated Pretraining Data	Contaminated Fine-tuning Data	ROUGE-1	ROUGE-2	ROUGE-L	ROUGE-LSUM
CNN	ZERO-SHOT	-	-	21.98 ± 0.26	5.076 ± 0.01	13.63 ± 0.10	18.51 ± 0.10
	BASELINE	-	×	27.22 ± 0.53	7.436 ± 0.13	18.15 ± 0.43	24.90 ± 0.36
	CHEATING	-	✓	**33.60** ± 0.58	**10.198** ± 0.16	**20.52** ± 0.33	**29.61** ± 0.32
	VERBATIM	✓	×	29.84 ± 0.48	9.488 ± 0.14	19.50 ± 0.38	26.98 ± 0.40
	DISTRIBUTION	✓	×	29.73 ± 0.33	*9.557* ± 0.13	*19.50* ± 0.22	27.12 ± 0.26
	MASKED	✓	×	28.34 ± 0.22	8.326 ± 0.13	18.01 ± 0.29	25.96 ± 0.20
	NOISED	✓	×	*31.31* ± 0.52	8.821 ± 0.15	19.19 ± 0.32	*28.85* ± 0.30
	REFORMATTED	✓	×	29.21 ± 0.28	8.887 ± 0.13	18.88 ± 0.29	26.27 ± 0.30
	INDOMAIN-VERBATIM	×	×	29.81 ± 0.48	9.277 ± 0.13	18.93 ± 0.25	26.88 ± 0.31
	INDOMAIN-DIST.	×	×	28.86 ± 0.30	8.910 ± 0.13	18.41 ± 0.27	26.10 ± 0.30
	INDOMAIN-MASK	×	×	28.87 ± 0.39	8.493 ± 0.15	18.24 ± 0.30	26.40 ± 0.29
	INDOMAIN-NOISE	×	×	31.16 ± 0.42	8.596 ± 0.10	18.85 ± 0.26	26.53 ± 0.35
	INDOMAIN-REFORM.	×	×	28.80 ± 0.31	8.681 ± 0.12	18.75 ± 0.24	26.07 ± 0.32
SAMSum	ZERO-SHOT	-	-	11.73 ± 0.14	1.357 ± 0.01	8.377 ± 0.19	9.331 ± 0.16
	BASELINE	-	×	32.95 ± 0.57	10.22 ± 0.15	25.83 ± 0.32	25.59 ± 0.29
	CHEATING	-	✓	**36.36** ± 0.53	**12.31** ± 0.14	**28.41** ± 0.33	**28.48** ± 0.33
	VERBATIM	✓	×	*34.34* ± 0.45	*10.76* ± 0.16	*26.98* ± 0.40	*27.04* ± 0.38
	DISTRIBUTION	✓	×	33.73 ± 0.51	10.32 ± 0.15	26.48 ± 0.31	26.56 ± 0.33
	MASKED	✓	×	33.05 ± 0.46	10.46 ± 0.15	25.77 ± 0.30	25.81 ± 0.28
	NOISED	✓	×	33.62 ± 0.43	10.27 ± 0.16	26.50 ± 0.37	26.49 ± 0.38
	REFORMATTED	✓	×	33.63 ± 0.39	10.25 ± 0.15	26.37 ± 0.31	26.46 ± 0.34
	INDOMAIN-VERBATIM	×	×	33.61 ± 0.46	10.27 ± 0.14	26.39 ± 0.30	26.46 ± 0.35
	INDOMAIN-DIST.	×	×	33.55 ± 0.42	10.26 ± 0.11	26.32 ± 0.33	26.44 ± 0.35
	INDOMAIN-MASK	×	×	32.87 ± 0.41	10.47 ± 0.12	25.74 ± 0.35	25.74 ± 0.31
	INDOMAIN-NOISE	×	×	33.67 ± 0.37	10.33 ± 0.13	26.38 ± 0.29	26.47 ± 0.28
	INDOMAIN-REFORM.	×	×	33.52 ± 0.34	10.24 ± 0.16	26.24 ± 0.28	26.34 ± 0.29
XSum	ZERO-SHOT	-	-	12.52 ± 0.11	2.059 ± 0.00	9.035 ± 0.16	10.27 ± 0.17
	BASELINE	-	×	26.28 ± 0.48	6.424 ± 0.12	19.80 ± 0.32	19.81 ± 0.33
	CHEATING	-	✓	**29.87** ± 0.41	**8.334** ± 0.13	**22.97** ± 0.43	**22.98** ± 0.42
	VERBATIM	✓	×	26.53 ± 0.51	6.820 ± 0.12	20.08 ± 0.33	20.03 ± 0.37
	DISTRIBUTION	✓	×	*26.61* ± 0.42	*6.885* ± 0.13	*20.12* ± 0.37	*20.11* ± 0.37
	MASKED	✓	×	24.50 ± 0.46	5.677 ± 0.12	18.16 ± 0.29	18.39 ± 0.31
	NOISED	✓	×	26.16 ± 0.39	6.599 ± 0.12	19.72 ± 0.35	19.72 ± 0.35
	REFORMATTED	✓	×	26.27 ± 0.43	6.623 ± 0.12	19.86 ± 0.29	19.86 ± 0.30
	INDOMAIN-VERBATIM	×	×	26.43 ± 0.41	6.745 ± 0.14	19.99 ± 0.27	19.99 ± 0.40
	INDOMAIN-DIST.	×	×	26.34 ± 0.40	6.666 ± 0.12	19.85 ± 0.32	19.85 ± 0.32
	INDOMAIN-MASK	×	×	24.31 ± 0.39	5.521 ± 0.13	18.02 ± 0.29	18.04 ± 0.34
	INDOMAIN-NOISE	×	×	26.31 ± 0.46	6.607 ± 0.11	19.80 ± 0.36	19.81 ± 0.28
	INDOMAIN-REFORM.	×	×	25.29 ± 0.32	6.280 ± 0.12	19.04 ± 0.35	19.06 ± 0.30

Table 3: Results for all 13 models trained on XSum, SAMSum, and CNN/Daily Mail Datasets. The table showcases evaluation metrics, with the best-performing model scores bolded and the second best italicized.

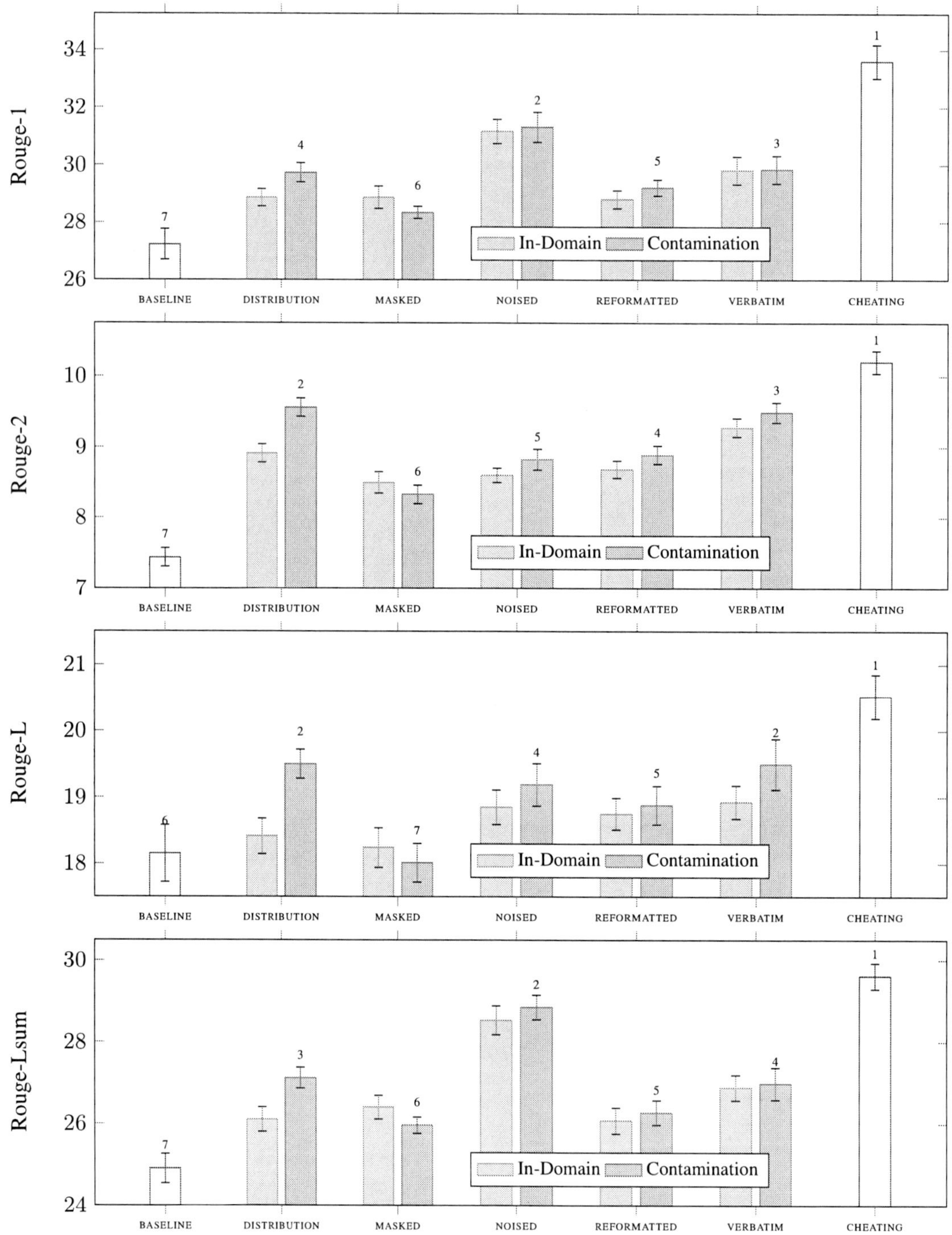

Figure 4: Bar Chart of all CNN/Daily Mail models compared for each metric

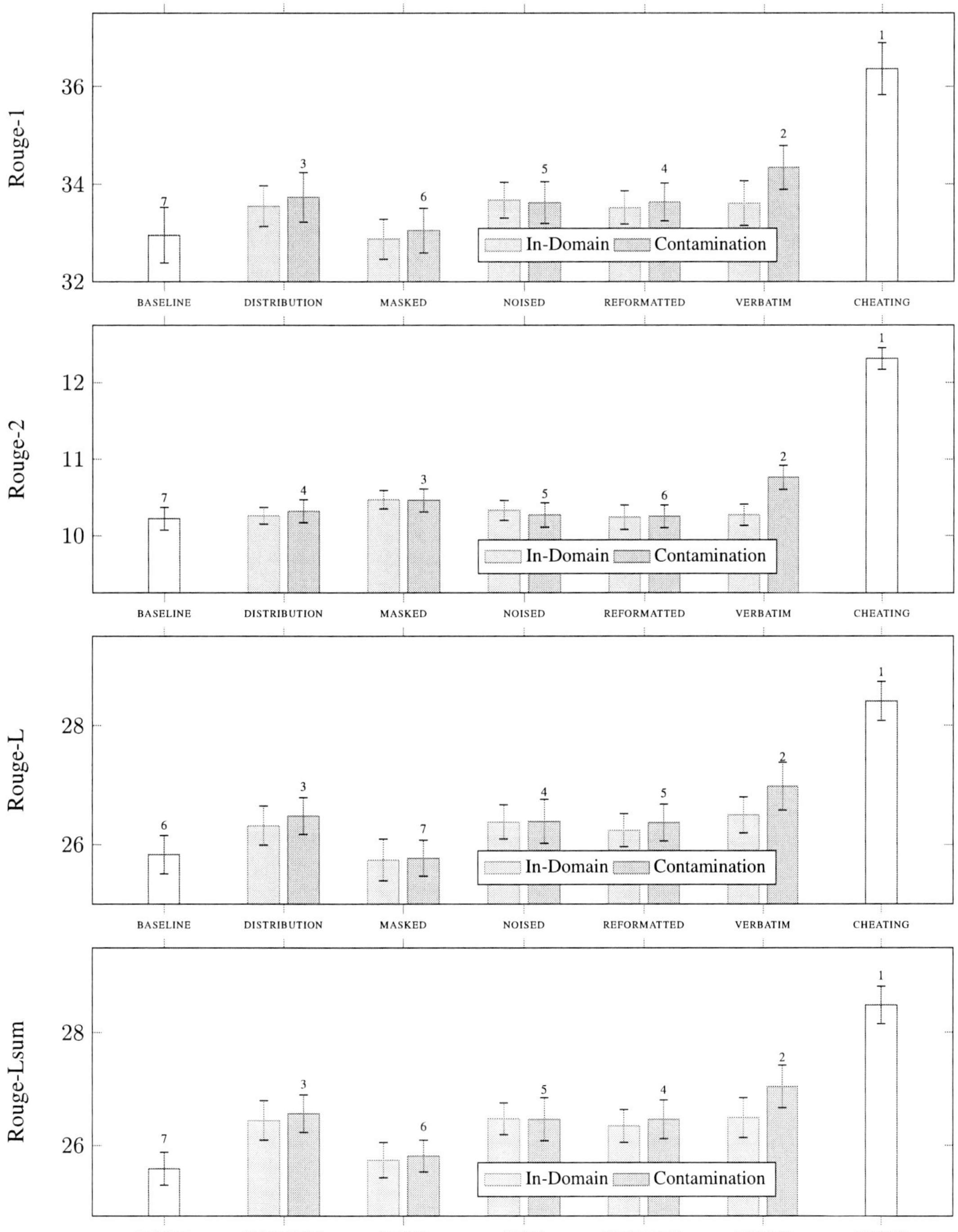

Figure 5: Bar Chart of all SAMSum models compared for each metric

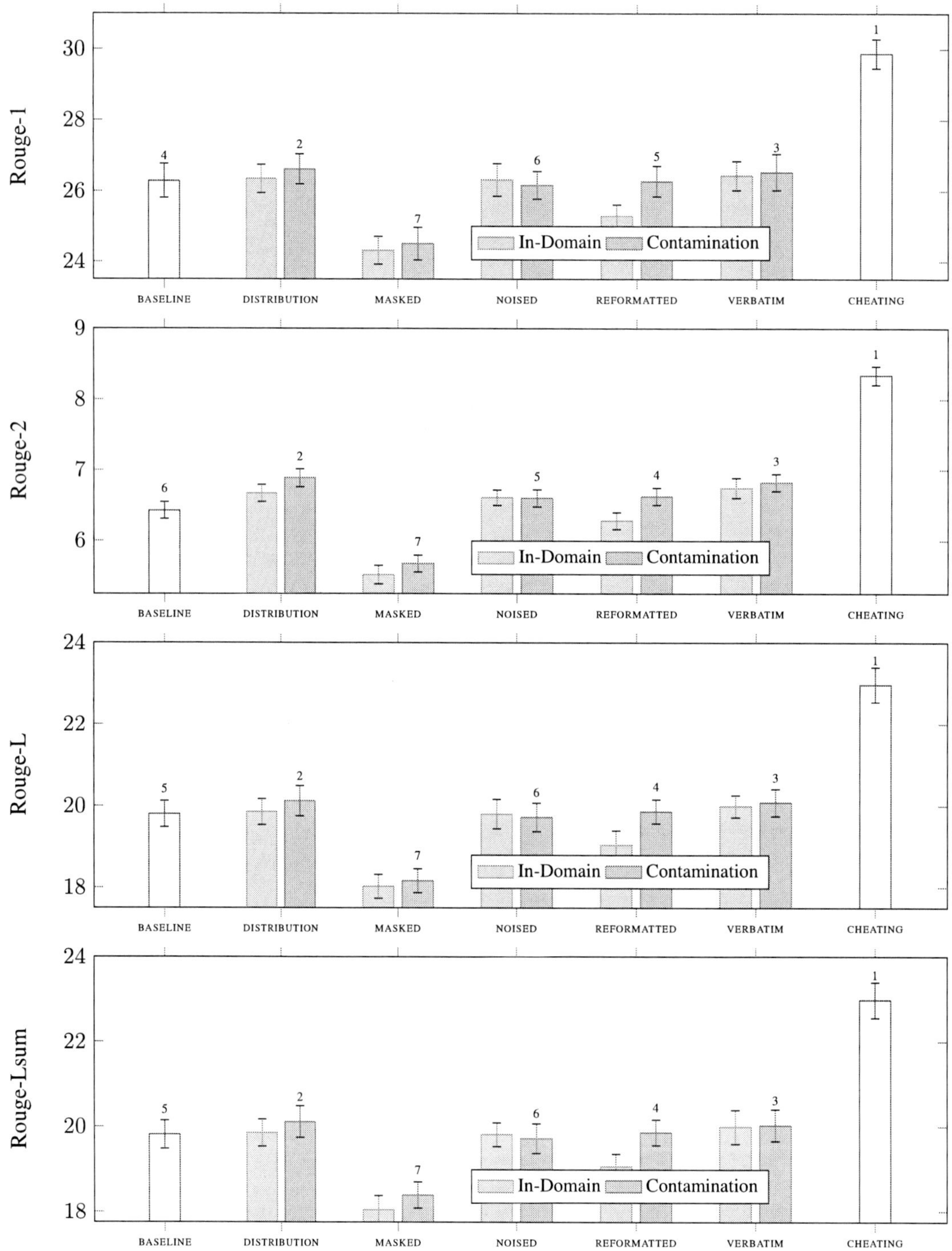

Figure 6: Bar Chart of all XSum models compared for each metric

B Full results for Question Answering Case Study

We present the full results of the QA case study. For each setting and dataset, we have included a table of the exact match and f1 metrics along with their standard deviations. The data is also presented through a series of bar charts for easier interpretability of the results for the reader. Standard deviations are measured over the results of the 3 models trained on random shuffles of the data.

Dataset	Model	Contaminated Pretraining Data	Contaminated Fine-tuning Data	Exact Match	F1 Score
SQuAD	ZERO-SHOT	-	-	1.178 ± 0.11	4.180 ± 0.22
	BASELINE	-	×	41.76 ± 1.01	55.72 ± 0.85
	CHEATING	-	✓	**55.73** ± 0.94	**66.47** ± 0.80
	VERBATIM	✓	×	53.38 ± 0.94	65.07 ± 0.96
	DISTRIBUTION	✓	×	52.76 ± 0.89	64.92 ± 0.88
	MASKED	✓	×	38.77 ± 0.96	51.93 ± 0.78
	NOISED	✓	×	52.72 ± 0.89	64.65 ± 0.89
	REFORMATTED	✓	×	48.08 ± 0.91	61.85 ± 0.94
	AUGMENTED	✓	×	*53.58* ± 0.98	*65.51* ± 0.90
	INDOMAIN-VERBATIM	×	×	52.44 ± 0.89	64.52 ± 0.92
	INDOMAIN-DIST.	×	×	51.90 ± 0.91	64.43 ± 0.87
	INDOMAIN-MASK	×	×	44.62 ± 0.93	58.95 ± 1.00
	INDOMAIN-NOISE	×	×	50.63 ± 0.85	63.60 ± 0.86
	INDOMAIN-REFORM.	×	×	51.30 ± 0.95	63.72 ± 0.95
	INDOMAIN-AUGMENT	×	×	52.94 ± 0.94	64.24 ± 0.89
CBT	ZERO-SHOT	-	-	1.192 ± 0.12	3.290 ± 0.21
	BASELINE	-	×	19.41 ± 0.99	19.84 ± 0.90
	CHEATING	-	✓	**54.27** ± 0.85	**56.39** ± 0.96
	VERBATIM	✓	×	*52.06* ± 0.88	*53.91* ± 0.89
	DISTRIBUTION	✓	×	50.82 ± 0.97	51.21 ± 0.97
	MASKED	✓	×	46.51 ± 0.84	47.43 ± 0.93
	NOISED	✓	×	49.59 ± 0.86	50.44 ± 0.96
	REFORMATTED	✓	×	51.46 ± 0.93	52.96 ± 0.86
	AUGMENTED	✓	×	49.09 ± 1.00	50.32 ± 0.89
	INDOMAIN-VERBATIM	×	×	44.19 ± 0.87	45.06 ± 0.96
	INDOMAIN-DIST.	×	×	42.85 ± 0.92	46.06 ± 0.90
	INDOMAIN-MASK	×	×	40.77 ± 0.96	40.18 ± 0.93
	INDOMAIN-NOISE	×	×	49.02 ± 0.97	49.11 ± 0.98
	INDOMAIN-REFORM.	×	×	50.01 ± 0.86	51.12 ± 0.86
	INDOMAIN-AUGMENT	×	×	50.46 ± 0.93	51.62 ± 0.84

Table 4: Results for all 15 models trained on the SQuAD and CBT dataset. The table showcases evaluation metrics, with the best-performing model scores bolded and the second best italicized.

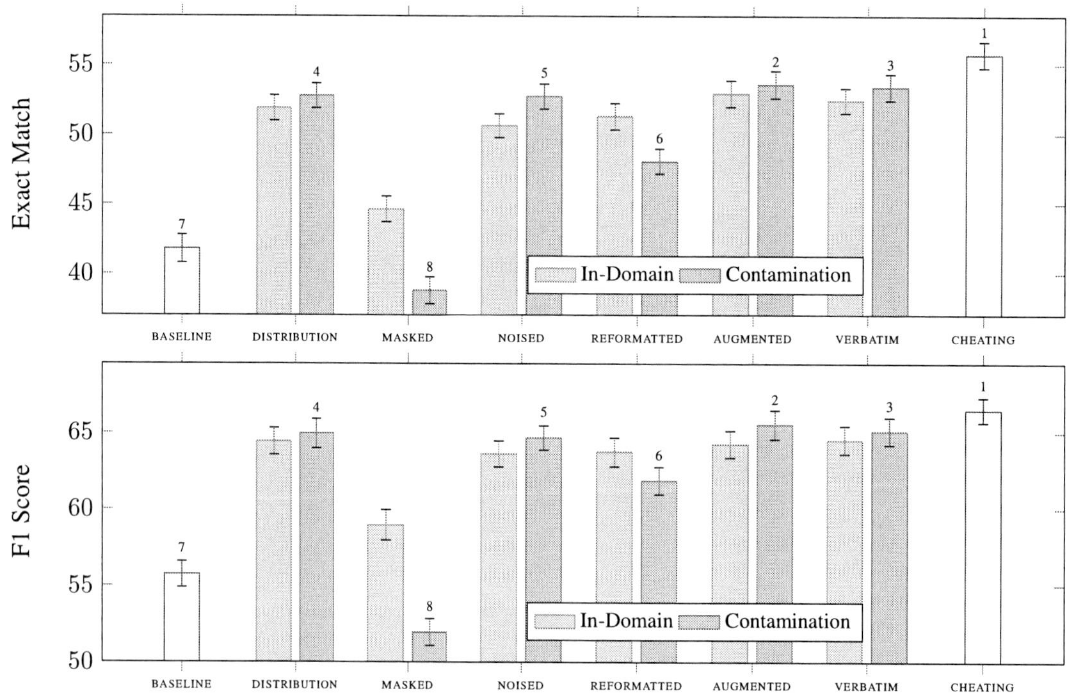

Figure 7: Bar Chart of all SQuAD models compared for each metric

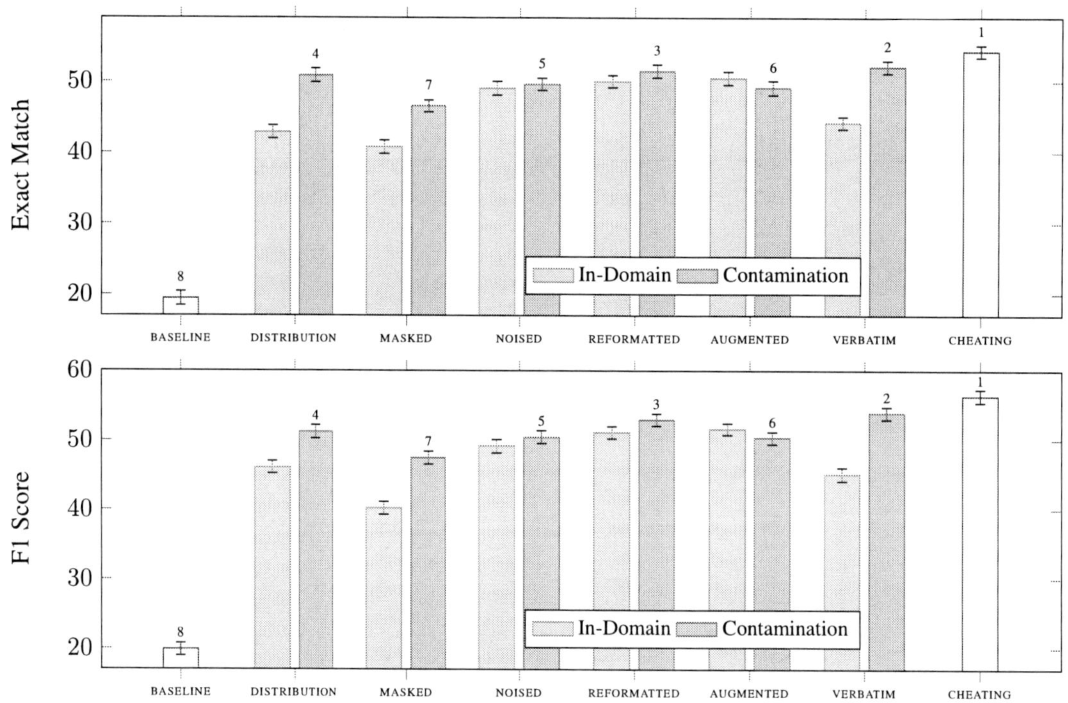

Figure 8: Bar Chart of all CBT models compared for each metric

C Examples for each contamination type

We provide examples of each of the functions from the different contamination types we are testing, applied to a sample from each dataset from the case studies.

Sample	Conversation: Anita: I'm at the station in Bologna Jenny: No problems so far? Anita: no, everything's going smoothly Tomy: good! Summary: Anita is at Bologna station.
Distribution	⟨ *some open web text* ⟩ Conversation: Anita: I'm at the station in Bologna Jenny: No problems so far? Anita: no, everything's going smoothly Tomy: good! Summary: Anita is at Bologna station. ⟨ *some more open web text* ⟩
Masking	Summary: Anita is at Bologna station.
Noising	Conversation: Anita: I'm at the station in Bologna Jenny: No problems so far? Anita: no, everything's going smoothly Tomy: good! Summary: Anita confirms her location at the Bologna station to Jenny and Tomy, reassuring them that everything is running smoothly.
Reformatting	Summary: Anita is at Bologna station. Conversation: Anita: I'm at the station in Bologna Jenny: No problems so far? Anita: no, everything's going smoothly Tomy: good!

Table 5: Applying the different contamination techniques to a sample from the SAMSum dataset.

Sample	Context: The Bey Hive is the name given to Beyoncé's fan base. Fans were previously titled "The Beyontourage", (a portmanteau of Beyoncé and entourage). The name Bey Hive derives from the word beehive, purposely misspelled to resemble her first name, and was penned by fans after petitions on the online social networking service Twitter and online news reports during competitions. Question: Beyonce has a fan base that is referred to as what? Answer: The Bey Hive
Distribution	⟨ *some open web text* ⟩ Context: The Bey Hive is the name given to Beyoncé's fan base. Fans were previously titled "The Beyontourage", (a portmanteau of Beyoncé and entourage). The name Bey Hive derives from the word beehive, purposely misspelled to resemble her first name, and was penned by fans after petitions on the online social networking service Twitter and online news reports during competitions. Question: Beyonce has a fan base that is referred to as what? Answer: The Bey Hive ⟨ *some more open web text* ⟩
Masking	Question: Beyonce has a fan base that is referred to as what? Answer: The Bey Hive
Noising	Context: The Bey Hive is the name given to Beyoncé's fan base. Fans were previously titled "The Beyontourage", (a portmanteau of Beyoncé and entourage). The name Bey Hive derives from the word beehive, purposely misspelled to resemble her first name, and was penned by fans after petitions on the online social networking service Twitter and online news reports during competitions. Question: Beyonce has a fan base that is referred to as what? Answer: Bey Hive
Reformatting	Context: The Bey Hive is the name given to Beyoncé's fan base. Fans were previously titled "The Beyontourage", (a portmanteau of Beyoncé and entourage). The name Bey Hive derives from the word beehive, purposely misspelled to resemble her first name, and was penned by fans after petitions on the online social networking service Twitter and online news reports during competitions. Question: Beyonce has a fan base that is referred to as what? Options: A) The Beehivers B) The Bey Hive C) The Beyontourage D) The Bey Flock Answer: The Bey Hive
Augmenting	Context: The Bey Hive is the name given to Beyoncé's fan base. Fans were previously titled "The Beyontourage", (a portmanteau of Beyoncé and entourage). The name Bey Hive derives from the word beehive, purposely misspelled to resemble her first name, and was penned by fans after petitions on the online social networking service Twitter and online news reports during competitions. This fervent fan base actively engages with Beyoncé's music, performances, and philanthropic endeavors. Question: Beyonce has a fan base that is referred to as what? Answer: The Bey Hive

Table 6: Applying the different contamination techniques to a sample from the SQuAD dataset.

Data Contamination Report from the 2024 CONDA Shared Task

Oscar Sainz[1] Iker García-Ferrero[1] Alon Jacovi[2]
Jon Ander Campos[3] Yanai Elazar[4,5] Eneko Agirre[1] Yoav Goldberg[2,4]

Wei-Lin Chen[6,7] Jenny Chim[8] Leshem Choshen[9,10] Luca D'Amico-Wong[11]
Melissa Dell[11] Run-Ze Fan[12] Shahriar Golchin[13] Yucheng Li[14] Pengfei Liu[12]
Bhavish Pahwa[15] Ameya Prabhu[17] Suryansh Sharma[18] Emily Silcock[11]
Kateryna Solonko[15] David Stap[19] Mihai Surdeanu[20] Yu-Min Tseng[21]
Vishaal Udandarao[16,17,22] Zengzhi Wang[12] Ruijie Xu[12] Jinglin Yang[11]

[1]HiTZ Center - Ixa, University of the Basque Country UPV/EHU [2]Bar Ilan University [3]Cohere
[4]Allen Institute for Artificial Intelligence [5]University of Washington [6]National Taiwan University
[7]University of Virginia [8]Queen Mary University of London [9]MIT-IBM Watson AI Lab [10]MIT
[11]Harvard University [12]Shanghai Jiao Tong University [13]University of Arizona [14]University of Surrey
[15]Microsoft Research [16]Tübingen AI Center [17]University of Tübingen
[18]Indian Institute of Technology Kharagpur [19]University of Amsterdam [20]University of Arizona
[21]Microsoft [22]University of Cambridge

Contact: conda-workshop@googlegroups.com

Abstract

The 1st Workshop on Data Contamination (CONDA 2024) focuses on all relevant aspects of data contamination in natural language processing, where data contamination is understood as situations where evaluation data is included in pre-training corpora used to train large scale models, compromising evaluation results. The workshop fostered a shared task to collect evidence on data contamination in current available datasets and models. The goal of the shared task and associated database is to assist the community in understanding the extent of the problem and to assist researchers in avoiding reporting evaluation results on known contaminated resources. The shared task provides a structured, centralized public database for the collection of contamination evidence, open to contributions from the community via GitHub pool requests. This first compilation paper is based on 566 reported entries over 91 contaminated sources from a total of 23 contributors. The details of the individual contamination events are available in the platform.[1] The platform continues to be online, open to contributions from the community.

1 Introduction

Data contamination, where evaluation data is inadvertently included in pre-training corpora of large-scale models, and language models (LMs) in particular, has become a concern in recent times (Sainz et al., 2023a; Jacovi et al., 2023). The growing scale of both models and data, coupled with massive web crawling, has led to the inclusion of segments from evaluation benchmarks in the pre-training data of LMs (Dodge et al., 2021; OpenAI et al., 2024; Anil et al., 2023; Elazar et al., 2024). The scale of internet data makes it difficult to prevent this contamination from happening, or even detect when it has happened (Bommasani et al., 2022; Mitchell et al., 2023).

Crucially, when evaluation data becomes part of pre-training data, it introduces biases and can artificially inflate the performance of LMs on specific tasks or benchmarks (Magar and Schwartz, 2022; Magnusson et al., 2023; Merrill et al., 2024). This poses a challenge for fair and unbiased evaluation of models, as their performance may not accurately reflect their generalization capabilities (Hupkes et al., 2023). And similarly to pre-training contamination, the contamination can also occur during the fine-tuning stage even *after* a model has been deployed as an API (Balloccu et al., 2024).

Although a growing number of papers and state-of-the-art models mention issues of data contamination (Brown et al., 2020; Wei et al., 2022; Chowdhery et al., 2022; OpenAI et al., 2024; Anil et al., 2023; Touvron et al., 2023), there is little in the way of organized and compiled knowledge about real, documented cases of contamination in practice (Sainz et al., 2023a). Addressing data contamination is a shared responsibility among researchers, developers, and the broader community.

Proceedings of the 1st Workshop on Data Contamination (CONDA), pages 41–56
August 16, 2024

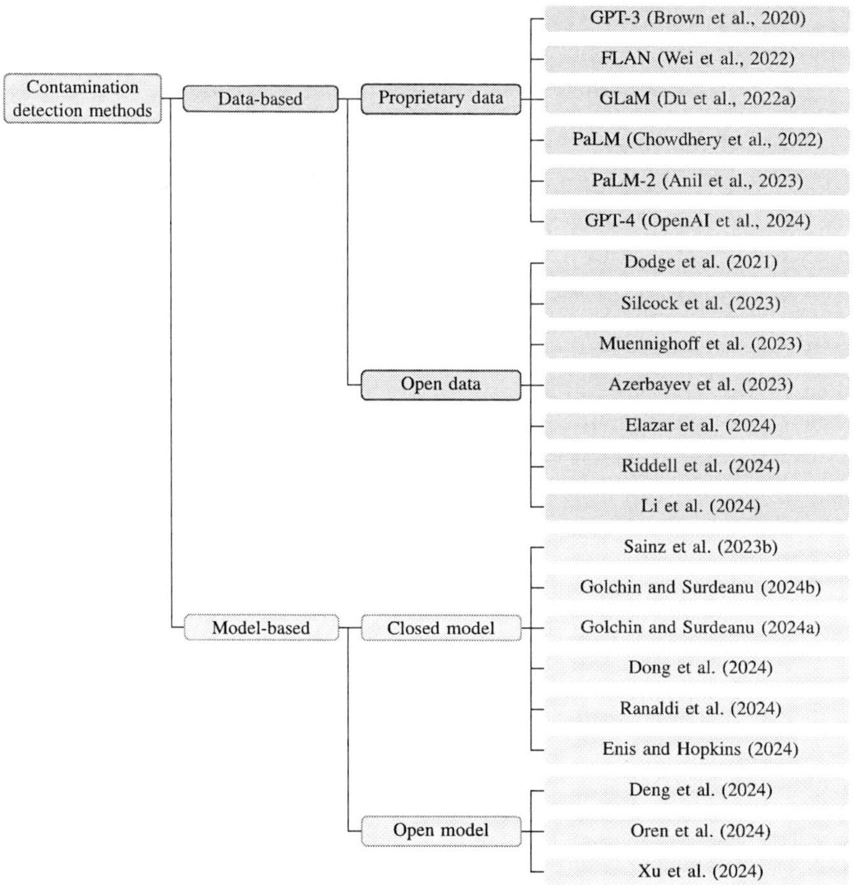

Figure 1: Taxonomy of papers that report contamination evidence. Including LLM's papers and technical reports, papers about methods for detecting contamination, and papers about corpus analysis.

This report compiles the evidence reported in the Data Contamination Database[1] as part of the Data Contamination Workshop.[2] As the Shared Task of the workshop, researchers were invited to discover cases of contamination in available corpora and models, and submit evidence of their discovery. The submissions to the database were collected and compiled on June 23rd, 2024, to be included in this report, but the database continues to run and grow. Overall we collected 566 submissions from 23 contributors, where each submission included a detailed contamination report, indicating the estimated percentage of contaminated data. We continue to operate the database, and expect to update it with newer datasets and models as they come out, as well as new report about existing contaminated (or uncontaminated) evaluations.

[1]https://huggingface.co/spaces/CONDA-Workshop/Data-Contamination-Database

[2]https://conda-workshop.github.io/

This report first presents the methodology for collecting evidence, as well as existing papers that report data contamination (Section 2). We also report the evidence collected in the Data Contamination Database (Section 3), followed by an overview of the trends and statistics in the database, that inform a high-level perspective on the state of data contamination in NLP today (Section 4).

2 Methodology and Previous Work

Collecting all the contamination evidence —or lack of it— was done openly, through pull requests, and subject to discussions before the admission. Contributors were asked to fill in the information about several aspects, such as the *contaminated resource* (a training corpus or model), the *evaluation dataset* which was found in the contaminated source, a breakdown of the percentage of contamination found in each split of the dataset (train, development, and test), an optional reference to a

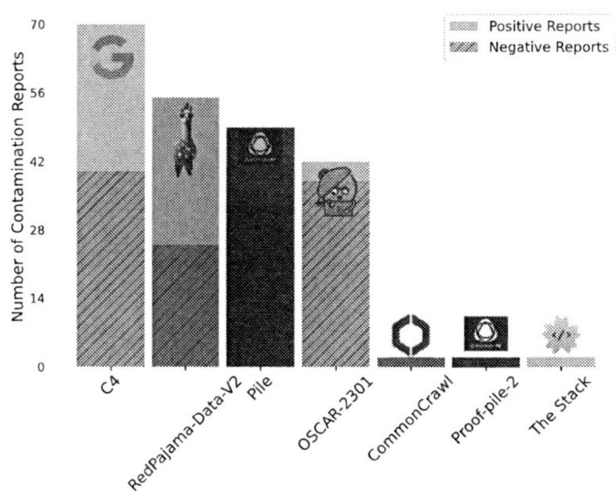

Figure 2: Number of test sets reported for each corpus often used in pre-training.

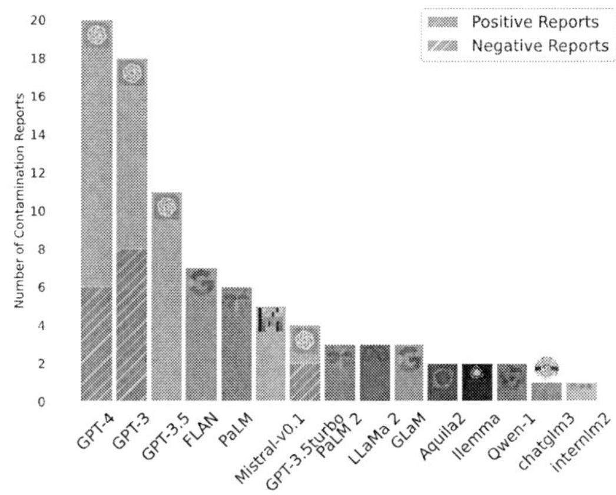

Figure 3: Number of test sets reported for each pre-trained model.

paper that describes the methodology behind the submission, as well as whether the contamination detection method was *data-based* or *model-based*. The contributions provided the HuggingFace Hub id of models, corpus, and datasets when possible. In addition, contributors must provide the evidence or a reference to the scientific paper that reported the evidence originally. Figure 1 shows the taxonomy of the papers that reported contamination evidence in the shared task.[3] We split the these methods into two: *data-based* and *model-based* approaches.

Data-based approaches. are methods that inspect the pre-training corpora to find contamination evidence. Data-based approaches typically involve string or sub-string matching techniques such as 13-gram overlap (Brown et al., 2020; Wei et al., 2022), 50-character overlap (OpenAI et al., 2024) or even full-string overlap (Elazar et al., 2024). In Figure 1 we differentiate between *Proprietary* and *Open* data. Papers that fall in the category of *Proprietary data* are usually LLMs technical reports that run post-hoc data contamination evaluations to identify and remove evaluation instances that appear in the pre-training corpora (Brown et al., 2020; Wei et al., 2022; OpenAI et al., 2024). Papers that fall in the *open data* category usually involve corpus analysis tools (Dodge et al., 2021; Elazar et al., 2024) or LLMs with publicly available pre-training data (Azerbayev et al., 2023).

Model-based approaches. are those methods that try to estimate the contamination of a model by prompting or analyzing the output, without accessing the pre-training data. These methods are formulated as Membership Inference Attacks (MIA) and range from asking LLMs to generate verbatim of the actual evaluation data (Sainz et al., 2023b; Golchin and Surdeanu, 2024b) to analyzing the actual output probabilities given by the model (Oren et al., 2024). We differentiate between methods applicable to *closed* and *open* models. Methods applicable to *closed* models are usually applicable to *open* models, but not the other way around due to the limitations established by the API or interface providers.

The collected evidences come from different approaches and sources, making them hardly comparable. For transparency, we included in the database information about the source of the evidence and the link to the discussion. We encourage the users to assess how the evidence was collected for their datasets of interest.

3 Compilation of Evidence

The report includes 42 contaminated sources (training corpora or models), 91 datasets, and 566 contamination entries, including 432 contamination events (20 train-set, 95 dev-set, 317 test-set) and 144 non-contamination events, where a contamination event is taken as any report above 0% of contamination. The database contains, for each split (train, dev, and test) of each evaluation dataset, what percentage was found to be contaminated by a subset of the contamination sources (corpora or models). We analyze separately the contaminated corpora and models.

[3] Note that there are many other works on data contamination detection. In this report we focus on works that were used to detect contamination for this report. We leave a more detailed coverage survey for future work.

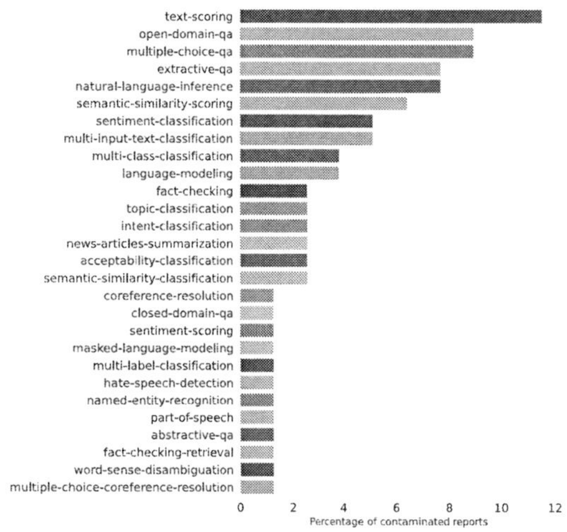

Figure 4: Percentage of contaminated report per task

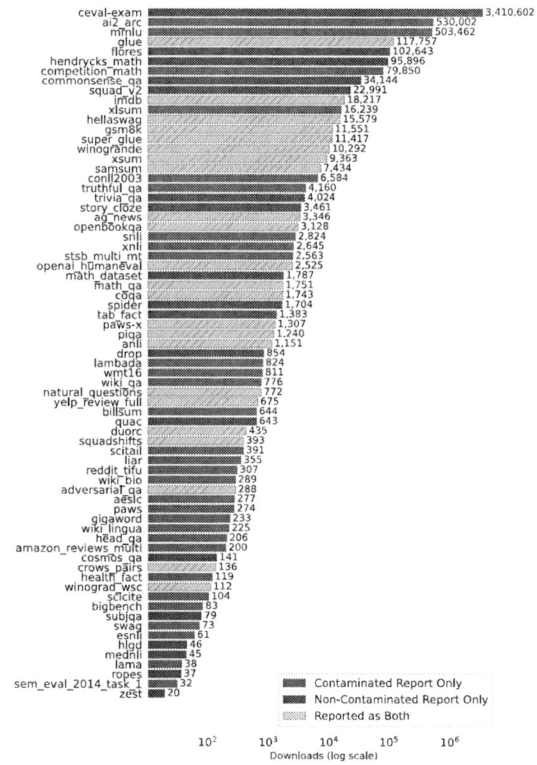

Figure 5: Number of downloads in the HuggingFace hub of the datasets in the report.

Contaminated corpora. Figure 2 shows the number of reported test sets for each corpus often used to pre-train language models. The reported corpora are mainly based on CommonCrawl snapshots, GitHub, or a mix of sources. For CommonCrawl-based corpora, there are 35 events reported for C4 (Raffel et al., 2023), 32 for RedPajama v2 (Computer, 2023), 29 for OSCAR (Jansen et al., 2022; Abadji et al., 2022, 2021; Kreutzer et al., 2022; Ortiz Su'arez et al., 2020; Ortiz Su'arez et al., 2019) and 6 for CommonCrawl (Rana, 2010) itself. Regarding the GitHub data, there are 2 events reported for the TheStack (Kocetkov et al., 2022) project. The corpora with various sources, the Pile (Gao et al., 2020) and ProofPile (Azerbayev et al., 2023), have 30 and 2 reported contamination events respectively. There is also 1 report for xP3 (Muennighoff et al., 2022), which is a collection of prompts for different NLP datasets.[4]

Table 1 shows for each corpus often used to pre-train language models, the contamination events involving development or test splits. Please refer to the online database for full details of each report.

Contaminated models. Figure 3 details the number of contamination events involving test sets that were reported, organised according to each pre-trained model. Most reported evidence is for closed models, for instance: 24 for GPT-3 (Brown et al., 2020), 17 for GLaM (Du et al., 2022a), 16 for GPT-4 (OpenAI et al., 2024), 13 for GPT-3.5 (Brown et al., 2020), 8 for PaLM (Chowdhery et al., 2022), 3 for PaLM-2 (Anil et al., 2023), 2 for GPT-3.5 Turbo (Brown et al., 2020) and 1 for Calude 3 Opus. In the case of open models: there are 14 reported events for models fine-tuned with FLAN data (Wei et al., 2022), 5 for Mistral (Jiang et al., 2023), 3 for Llama 2 (Touvron et al., 2023), 2 for Qwen (Bai et al., 2023), Llema (Azerbayev et al., 2023) and Aquila 2; and a single one for mT0 and Bloom-Z (Muennighoff et al., 2022).

Table 2 shows for each pre-trained language model, the contamination events involving development or test splits. Please refer to the online database for full details of each report.

4 Analysis of the Reported Data

In this section, we analyze the reported entries to understand the report's data better.

Reported tasks. Figure 4 shows the percentage of data contamination per task. We use the `task_id` assigned to each dataset in the Hugging Face hub. Text-scoring, QA, and multiple-choice-qa are among the most contaminated task types. Figure 5 shows the number of downloads for every dataset in the report. We measure the total num-

[4]The report indicates the use of validation data from a specific dataset as training.

Contaminated Source	Evaluation Set
allenai/c4 (Raffel et al., 2023),	sem_eval_2014_task_1 (Marelli et al., 2014), race, nyu-mll/glue (Wang et al., 2019b), amazon_reviews_multi (Keung et al., 2020), liar (Wang, 2017), reddit_tifu (Kim et al., 2018), stsb_multi_mt (May, 2021), wiki_qa (Yang et al., 2015), gigaword (Graff et al., 2003), piqa (Bisk et al., 2020), esnli (Camburu et al., 2018), scitail (Khot et al., 2018), snli (Bowman et al., 2015), ibm/duorc (Saha et al., 2018), math_qa (Amini et al., 2019), swag (Zellers et al., 2018), wiki_bio (Lebret et al., 2016), xnli (Conneau et al., 2018), allenai/scicite (Cohan et al., 2019), aeslc (Zhang and Tetreault, 2019), billsum (Kornilova and Eidelman, 2019), AMR-to-Text, winograd_wsc (Levesque et al., 2012), squadshifts (Miller et al., 2020), head_qa (Vilares and Gómez-Rodríguez, 2019), xsum (Narayan et al., 2018), health_fact (Kotonya and Toni, 2020), EdinburghNLP/xsum (Narayan et al., 2018), UCLNLP/adversarial_qa (Bartolo et al., 2020), paws (Zhang et al., 2019), sick, super_glue (Wang et al., 2019a), paws-x (Yang et al., 2019), scan, lama (Petroni et al., 2019, 2020)
CommonCrawl (Rana, 2010)	allenai/ai2_arc (Clark et al., 2018), tau/commonsense_qa (Talmor et al., 2019), ceval/ceval-exam (Huang et al., 2023), cais/mmlu (Hendrycks et al., 2021a), Rowan/hellaswag (Zellers et al., 2019), winogrande (Levesque et al., 2012)
EleutherAI/pile (Gao et al., 2020)	sem_eval_2014_task_1 (Marelli et al., 2014), nyu-mll/glue (Wang et al., 2019b), amazon_reviews_multi (Keung et al., 2020), mbpp, openai_humaneval (Chen et al., 2021), liar (Wang, 2017), stsb_multi_mt (May, 2021), wiki_qa (Yang et al., 2015), gigaword (Graff et al., 2003), piqa (Bisk et al., 2020), esnli (Camburu et al., 2018), scitail (Khot et al., 2018), snli (Bowman et al., 2015), ibm/duorc (Saha et al., 2018), swag (Zellers et al., 2018), xnli (Conneau et al., 2018), allenai/scicite (Cohan et al., 2019), aeslc (Zhang and Tetreault, 2019), billsum (Kornilova and Eidelman, 2019), winograd_wsc (Levesque et al., 2012), squadshifts (Miller et al., 2020), head_qa (Vilares and Gómez-Rodríguez, 2019), xsum (Narayan et al., 2018), health_fact (Kotonya and Toni, 2020), UCLNLP/adversarial_qa (Bartolo et al., 2020), paws (Zhang et al., 2019), sick, super_glue (Wang et al., 2019a), paws-x (Yang et al., 2019), scan
oscar-corpus/OSCAR-2301 (Jansen et al., 2022; Abadji et al., 2022, 2021; Kreutzer et al., 2022; Ortiz Su'arez et al., 2020; Ortiz Su'arez et al., 2019)	sem_eval_2014_task_1 (Marelli et al., 2014), crows_pairs (Nangia et al., 2020), nyu-mll/glue (Wang et al., 2019b), race, amazon_reviews_multi (Keung et al., 2020), openai_humaneval (Chen et al., 2021), liar (Wang, 2017), stsb_multi_mt (May, 2021), wiki_qa (Yang et al., 2015), gigaword (Graff et al., 2003), piqa (Bisk et al., 2020), esnli (Camburu et al., 2018), scitail (Khot et al., 2018), snli (Bowman et al., 2015), math_qa (Amini et al., 2019), swag (Zellers et al., 2018), xnli (Conneau et al., 2018), allenai/scicite (Cohan et al., 2019), aeslc (Zhang and Tetreault, 2019), billsum (Kornilova and Eidelman, 2019), winograd_wsc (Levesque et al., 2012), squadshifts (Miller et al., 2020), head_qa (Vilares and Gómez-Rodríguez, 2019), xsum (Narayan et al., 2018), health_fact (Kotonya and Toni, 2020), UCLNLP/adversarial_qa (Bartolo et al., 2020), paws (Zhang et al., 2019), sick, super_glue (Wang et al., 2019a)
togethercomputer/RedPajama-Data-V2 (Computer, 2023)	sem_eval_2014_task_1 (Marelli et al., 2014), race, nyu-mll/glue (Wang et al., 2019b), amazon_reviews_multi (Keung et al., 2020), liar (Wang, 2017), stsb_multi_mt (May, 2021), wiki_qa (Yang et al., 2015), gigaword (Graff et al., 2003), piqa (Bisk et al., 2020), esnli (Camburu et al., 2018), scitail (Khot et al., 2018), snli (Bowman et al., 2015), ibm/duorc (Saha et al., 2018), math_qa (Amini et al., 2019), swag (Zellers et al., 2018), xnli (Conneau et al., 2018), allenai/scicite (Cohan et al., 2019), aeslc (Zhang and Tetreault, 2019), billsum (Kornilova and Eidelman, 2019), winograd_wsc (Levesque et al., 2012), squadshifts (Miller et al., 2020), head_qa (Vilares and Gómez-Rodríguez, 2019), xsum (Narayan et al., 2018), health_fact (Kotonya and Toni, 2020), UCLNLP/adversarial_qa (Bartolo et al., 2020), mc_taco, paws (Zhang et al., 2019), samsum (Gliwa et al., 2019), sick, super_glue (Wang et al., 2019a), paws-x (Yang et al., 2019), scan
bigscience/xP3 (Muennighoff et al., 2022)	facebook/flores (NLLB-Team et al., 2022)
EleutherAI/proof-pile-2 (Azerbayev et al., 2023)	gsm8k (Cobbe et al., 2021), hendrycks/competition_math (Hendrycks et al., 2021b)
bigcode/the-stack (Kocetkov et al., 2022)	openai_humaneval (Chen et al., 2021), mbpp

Table 1: A summary of the *dev* or *test* sets found at above 0% contamination in each corpus often used to pre-train models.

ber of downloads from the Hugging Face hub.[5] Since one model may be reported as contaminated with a dataset while another model may not, we have entries of both being compromised and non-compromised for some datasets. Relating both tables, we can see that the tasks reported as the most contaminated include very popular datasets such as MMLU (multiple-choice-qa), GLUE (text-scoring), and ai2_arc (multiple-choice-qa), which are standard benchmarks for measuring the performance of LLMs. These benchmarks, as well as other very popular benchmarks reported in instances of data contamination, such as hellaswag or gsm8k are implemented in community leaderboards such as the Open LLM Leaderboard.[6]

Year of publication of the reported data. Figure 7 shows the percentage of total test sets included in contamination events per year. We present data

[5] https://huggingface.co/docs/datasets

[6] https://hf.co/spaces/open-llm-leaderboard/

Contaminated Source	Evaluation Set
GPT-3 (Brown et al., 2020)	Reversed Words , race , quac (Choi et al., 2018), Anagrams 1 , Cycled Letters , mandarjoshi/trivia_qa (Joshi et al., 2017), ibragim-bad/arc_easy (Clark et al., 2018), SAT Analogies, piqa (Bisk et al., 2020), Rowan/hellaswag (Zellers et al., 2019), wmt/wmt16 (Bojar et al., 2016), stanfordnlp/coqa (Reddy et al., 2019), cimec/lambada (Paperno et al., 2016), natural_questions (Kwiatkowski et al., 2019), winograd_wsc (Levesque et al., 2012), ucinlp/drop (Dua et al., 2019), rmanluo/RoG-webqsp, rajpurkar/squad_v2 (Rajpurkar et al., 2018, 2016), allenai/openbookqa (Mihaylov et al., 2018), Symbol Insertion, Anagrams 2 , super_glue (Wang et al., 2019a), ibragim-bad/arc_challenge (Clark et al., 2018), facebook/anli (Nie et al., 2020)
GPT-3.5 (Brown et al., 2020)	samsum (Gliwa et al., 2019), yelp_review_full (Zhang et al., 2015a), imdb (Maas et al., 2011), ag_news (Zhang et al., 2015b), nyu-mll/glue (Wang et al., 2019b), conll2003 (Tjong Kim Sang and De Meulder, 2003), winogrande (Levesque et al., 2012), rajpurkar/squad_v2 (Rajpurkar et al., 2018, 2016), cais/mmlu (Hendrycks et al., 2021a), EdinburghNLP/xsum (Narayan et al., 2018), allenai/openbookqa (Mihaylov et al., 2018), xlangai/spider (Yu et al., 2018), truthful_qa (Lin et al., 2022)
GPT-4 (OpenAI et al., 2024)	samsum (Gliwa et al., 2019), yelp_review_full (Zhang et al., 2015a), gsm8k (Cobbe et al., 2021), imdb (Maas et al., 2011), ibragim-bad/arc_challenge (Clark et al., 2018), nyu-mll/glue (Wang et al., 2019b), ucinlp/drop (Dua et al., 2019), winogrande (Levesque et al., 2012), openai_humaneval (Chen et al., 2021), ag_news (Zhang et al., 2015b), EdinburghNLP/xsum (Narayan et al., 2018), cais/mmlu (Hendrycks et al., 2021a), Rowan/hellaswag (Zellers et al., 2019), allenai/openbookqa (Mihaylov et al., 2018), truthful_qa (Lin et al., 2022), bigbench (Srivastava et al., 2023)
PaLM 2 (Anil et al., 2023)	EdinburghNLP/xsum (Narayan et al., 2018), csebuetnlp/xlsum (Hasan et al., 2021), wiki_lingua (Ladhak et al., 2020)
GPT-3.5-turbo (Brown et al., 2020)	openai_humaneval (Chen et al., 2021), HumanEval_R (Chen et al., 2021)
FLAN (Wei et al., 2022)	natural_questions (Kwiatkowski et al., 2019), mandarjoshi/trivia_qa (Joshi et al., 2017), story_cloze (Sharma et al., 2018), piqa (Bisk et al., 2020), super_glue (Wang et al., 2019a), ibragim-bad/arc_challenge (Clark et al., 2018), ucinlp/drop (Dua et al., 2019), rajpurkar/squad_v2 (Rajpurkar et al., 2018, 2016), ibragim-bad/arc_easy (Clark et al., 2018), Rowan/hellaswag (Zellers et al., 2019), allenai/openbookqa (Mihaylov et al., 2018), facebook/anli (Nie et al., 2020), winogrande (Levesque et al., 2012), wmt/wmt16 (Bojar et al., 2016)
GLaM (Du et al., 2022a)	stanfordnlp/coqa (Reddy et al., 2019), natural_questions (Kwiatkowski et al., 2019), mandarjoshi/trivia_qa (Joshi et al., 2017), story_cloze (Sharma et al., 2018), cimec/lambada (Paperno et al., 2016), piqa (Bisk et al., 2020), super_glue (Wang et al., 2019a), ibragim-bad/arc_challenge (Clark et al., 2018), race , quac (Choi et al., 2018), winograd_wsc (Levesque et al., 2012), rajpurkar/squad_v2 (Rajpurkar et al., 2018, 2016), ibragim-bad/arc_easy (Clark et al., 2018), Rowan/hellaswag (Zellers et al., 2019), allenai/openbookqa (Mihaylov et al., 2018), facebook/anli (Nie et al., 2020), winogrande (Levesque et al., 2012)
LLaMa 2-13B (Touvron et al., 2023)	allenai/openbookqa (Mihaylov et al., 2018), winogrande (Levesque et al., 2012), truthful_qa (Lin et al., 2022)
Mistral-7B (Jiang et al., 2023)	allenai/openbookqa (Mihaylov et al., 2018), winogrande (Levesque et al., 2012), truthful_qa (Lin et al., 2022), cais/mmlu (Hendrycks et al., 2021a)
PaLM (Chowdhery et al., 2022)	cimec/lambada (Paperno et al., 2016), super_glue (Wang et al., 2019a), ibragim-bad/arc_challenge (Clark et al., 2018), winograd_wsc (Levesque et al., 2012), rmanluo/RoG-webqsp, rajpurkar/squad_v2 (Rajpurkar et al., 2018, 2016), mandarjoshi/trivia_qa (Joshi et al., 2017), ibragim-bad/arc_easy (Clark et al., 2018)
Claude 3 Opus	facebook/flores (NLLB-Team et al., 2022)
bigscience/bloomz (Muennighoff et al., 2022)	facebook/flores (NLLB-Team et al., 2022)
bigscience/mt0-* (Muennighoff et al., 2022)	facebook/flores (NLLB-Team et al., 2022)
BAAI/Aquila2-34B	gsm8k (Cobbe et al., 2021), hendrycks/competition_math (Hendrycks et al., 2021b)
BAAI/AquilaChat2-34B	gsm8k (Cobbe et al., 2021)
EleutherAI/llemma_* (Azerbayev et al., 2023)	gsm8k (Cobbe et al., 2021), hendrycks/competition_math (Hendrycks et al., 2021b)
Qwen/Qwen-1_8B (Bai et al., 2023)	gsm8k (Cobbe et al., 2021), hendrycks/competition_math (Hendrycks et al., 2021b)
BAAI/Aquila2-7B	hendrycks/competition_math (Hendrycks et al., 2021b)
Qwen/Qwen-* (Bai et al., 2023)	hendrycks/competition_math (Hendrycks et al., 2021b)
THUDM/chatglm3-6b (Du et al., 2022b)	hendrycks/competition_math (Hendrycks et al., 2021b)
internlm/internlm2-* (Cai et al., 2024)	hendrycks/competition_math (Hendrycks et al., 2021b)
mistralai/Mistral-7B-v0.1 (Jiang et al., 2023)	ibragim-bad/arc_easy (Clark et al., 2018)

Table 2: A summary of the *dev* or *test* sets found at above 0% contamination in each reported model. The "*" is used to indicate the different versions or sizes of the models.

for test sets in both contamination events (>0% contamination) and non-contamination events (0% contamination). Most of the reported datasets correspond to the 2018 to 2021 period.

We further explore the relationship between the year of publication of the datasets and instances of contamination by examining the reported data contamination for the three models with the most instances of data contamination: GPT-4, GPT-3, and GPT-3.5. As expected based on the models' release dates, Figure 6 shows that more recently released models are contaminated with more recently released datasets. For instance, GPT-3, launched in 2020, is predominantly contaminated with datasets from 2016, while GPT-4, released in 2023, is mainly contaminated with datasets from 2018 to 2022.

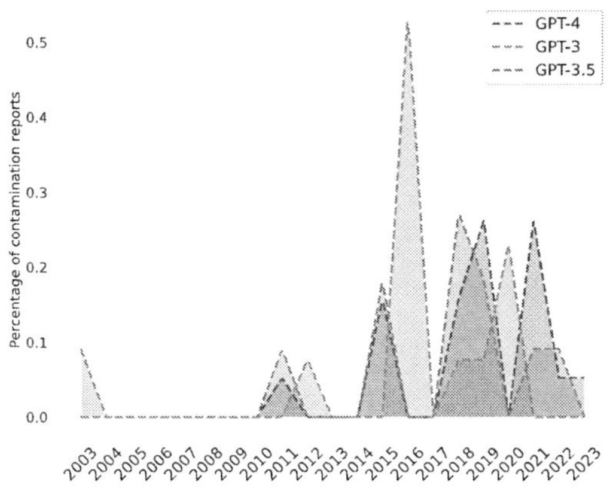

Figure 6: Year of publication of the contaminated test sets reported for each model.

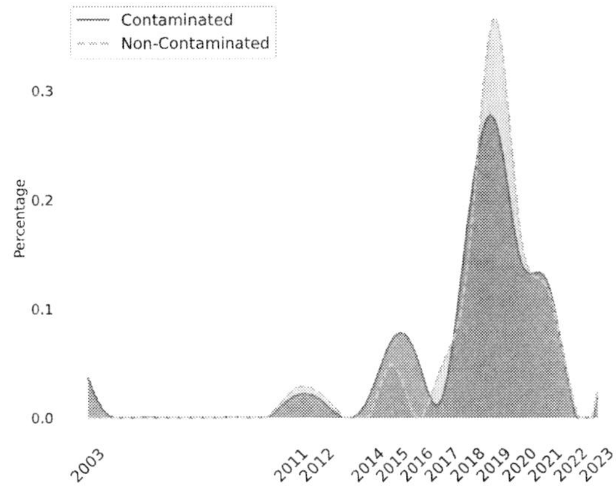

Figure 7: Publication year of the test sets included in the data contamination report.

5 Conclusions

Data contamination has become a significant concern in recent times. Consequently, a growing number of papers and state-of-the-art models mention issues of data contamination. In the CONDA 2024 Shared Task on Evidence of Data Contamination, we have collected and compiled a comprehensive database of available evidence on data contamination in currently available datasets and models. This report includes 566 contamination entries over 91 contaminated sources from a total of 23 contributors. With this shared task, we provide a structured, centralized platform for contamination evidence collection to help the community understand the extent of the problem and to assist researchers in avoiding reporting evaluation results on known contaminated resources. Given the large exploration space, this report does not cover all cases, but a small sample that were reported during our shared task period, in the midst of 2024. We welcome further submissions to the database, and plan to keep this database up-to-date as it provides a valuable source of information for the research community.

Acknowledgments

We are grateful to Hugging Face and Clémentine Fourrier for their support in establishing the website for the Data Contamination Database hosted on Hugging Face Spaces. We acknowledge the support of project Disargue (TED2021-130810B-C21, funded by MCIN/AEI /10.13039/501100011033 and by European Union NextGenerationEU/ PRTR) and the Basque Government (Research group funding IT-1805-22).

References

Julien Abadji, Pedro Ortiz Suarez, Laurent Romary, and Benoît Sagot. 2022. Towards a cleaner document-oriented multilingual crawled corpus. In *Proceedings of the Thirteenth Language Resources and Evaluation Conference*, pages 4344–4355, Marseille, France. European Language Resources Association.

Julien Abadji, Pedro Javier Ortiz Suárez, Laurent Romary, and Benoît Sagot. 2021. Ungoliant: An optimized pipeline for the generation of a very large-scale multilingual web corpus. Proceedings of the Workshop on Challenges in the Management of Large Corpora (CMLC-9) 2021. Limerick, 12 July 2021 (Online-Event), pages 1 – 9, Mannheim. Leibniz-Institut für Deutsche Sprache.

Aida Amini, Saadia Gabriel, Shanchuan Lin, Rik Koncel-Kedziorski, Yejin Choi, and Hannaneh Hajishirzi. 2019. MathQA: Towards interpretable math word problem solving with operation-based formalisms. In *Proceedings of the 2019 Conference of the North American Chapter of the Association for Computational Linguistics: Human Language Technologies, Volume 1 (Long and Short Papers)*, pages 2357–2367, Minneapolis, Minnesota. Association for Computational Linguistics.

Rohan Anil, Andrew M. Dai, Orhan Firat, Melvin Johnson, Dmitry Lepikhin, Alexandre Passos, Siamak Shakeri, Emanuel Taropa, Paige Bailey, Zhifeng Chen, Eric Chu, Jonathan H. Clark, Laurent El Shafey, Yanping Huang, Kathy Meier-Hellstern, Gaurav Mishra, Erica Moreira, Mark Omernick, Kevin Robinson, Sebastian Ruder, Yi Tay, Kefan Xiao, Yuanzhong Xu, Yujing Zhang, Gustavo Hernandez Abrego, Junwhan Ahn, Jacob Austin, Paul Barham, Jan Botha, James Bradbury, Siddhartha Brahma, Kevin Brooks, Michele Catasta, Yong Cheng, Colin Cherry, Christopher A. Choquette-Choo, Aakanksha Chowdhery, Clément Crepy, Shachi Dave, Mostafa Dehghani, Sunipa Dev, Jacob Devlin, Mark Díaz, Nan Du, Ethan Dyer, Vlad Feinberg, Fangxiaoyu

Feng, Vlad Fienber, Markus Freitag, Xavier Garcia, Sebastian Gehrmann, Lucas Gonzalez, Guy Gur-Ari, Steven Hand, Hadi Hashemi, Le Hou, Joshua Howland, Andrea Hu, Jeffrey Hui, Jeremy Hurwitz, Michael Isard, Abe Ittycheriah, Matthew Jagielski, Wenhao Jia, Kathleen Kenealy, Maxim Krikun, Sneha Kudugunta, Chang Lan, Katherine Lee, Benjamin Lee, Eric Li, Music Li, Wei Li, YaGuang Li, Jian Li, Hyeontaek Lim, Hanzhao Lin, Zhongtao Liu, Frederick Liu, Marcello Maggioni, Aroma Mahendru, Joshua Maynez, Vedant Misra, Maysam Moussalem, Zachary Nado, John Nham, Eric Ni, Andrew Nystrom, Alicia Parrish, Marie Pellat, Martin Polacek, Alex Polozov, Reiner Pope, Siyuan Qiao, Emily Reif, Bryan Richter, Parker Riley, Alex Castro Ros, Aurko Roy, Brennan Saeta, Rajkumar Samuel, Renee Shelby, Ambrose Slone, Daniel Smilkov, David R. So, Daniel Sohn, Simon Tokumine, Dasha Valter, Vijay Vasudevan, Kiran Vodrahalli, Xuezhi Wang, Pidong Wang, Zirui Wang, Tao Wang, John Wieting, Yuhuai Wu, Kelvin Xu, Yunhan Xu, Linting Xue, Pengcheng Yin, Jiahui Yu, Qiao Zhang, Steven Zheng, Ce Zheng, Weikang Zhou, Denny Zhou, Slav Petrov, and Yonghui Wu. 2023. Palm 2 technical report. *Preprint*, arXiv:2305.10403.

Zhangir Azerbayev, Hailey Schoelkopf, Keiran Paster, Marco Dos Santos, Stephen McAleer, Albert Q. Jiang, Jia Deng, Stella Biderman, and Sean Welleck. 2023. Llemma: An open language model for mathematics. *Preprint*, arXiv:2310.10631.

Jinze Bai, Shuai Bai, Yunfei Chu, Zeyu Cui, Kai Dang, Xiaodong Deng, Yang Fan, Wenbin Ge, Yu Han, Fei Huang, Binyuan Hui, Luo Ji, Mei Li, Junyang Lin, Runji Lin, Dayiheng Liu, Gao Liu, Chengqiang Lu, Keming Lu, Jianxin Ma, Rui Men, Xingzhang Ren, Xuancheng Ren, Chuanqi Tan, Sinan Tan, Jianhong Tu, Peng Wang, Shijie Wang, Wei Wang, Shengguang Wu, Benfeng Xu, Jin Xu, An Yang, Hao Yang, Jian Yang, Shusheng Yang, Yang Yao, Bowen Yu, Hongyi Yuan, Zheng Yuan, Jianwei Zhang, Xingxuan Zhang, Yichang Zhang, Zhenru Zhang, Chang Zhou, Jingren Zhou, Xiaohuan Zhou, and Tianhang Zhu. 2023. Qwen technical report. *arXiv preprint arXiv:2309.16609*.

Simone Balloccu, Patrícia Schmidtová, Mateusz Lango, and Ondrej Dusek. 2024. Leak, cheat, repeat: Data contamination and evaluation malpractices in closed-source LLMs. In *Proceedings of the 18th Conference of the European Chapter of the Association for Computational Linguistics (Volume 1: Long Papers)*, pages 67–93, St. Julian's, Malta. Association for Computational Linguistics.

Max Bartolo, Alastair Roberts, Johannes Welbl, Sebastian Riedel, and Pontus Stenetorp. 2020. Beat the ai: Investigating adversarial human annotation for reading comprehension. *Transactions of the Association for Computational Linguistics*, 8:662–678.

Yonatan Bisk, Rowan Zellers, Ronan Le Bras, Jianfeng Gao, and Yejin Choi. 2020. Piqa: Reasoning about physical commonsense in natural language. In *Thirty-Fourth AAAI Conference on Artificial Intelligence*.

Ond rej Bojar, Rajen Chatterjee, Christian Federmann, Yvette Graham, Barry Haddow, Matthias Huck, Antonio Jimeno Yepes, Philipp Koehn, Varvara Logacheva, Christof Monz, Matteo Negri, Aurelie Neveol, Mariana Neves, Martin Popel, Matt Post, Raphael Rubino, Carolina Scarton, Lucia Specia, Marco Turchi, Karin Verspoor, and Marcos Zampieri. 2016. Findings of the 2016 conference on machine translation. In *Proceedings of the First Conference on Machine Translation*, pages 131–198, Berlin, Germany. Association for Computational Linguistics.

Rishi Bommasani, Drew A. Hudson, Ehsan Adeli, Russ Altman, Simran Arora, Sydney von Arx, Michael S. Bernstein, Jeannette Bohg, Antoine Bosselut, Emma Brunskill, Erik Brynjolfsson, Shyamal Buch, Dallas Card, Rodrigo Castellon, Niladri Chatterji, Annie Chen, Kathleen Creel, Jared Quincy Davis, Dora Demszky, Chris Donahue, Moussa Doumbouya, Esin Durmus, Stefano Ermon, John Etchemendy, Kawin Ethayarajh, Li Fei-Fei, Chelsea Finn, Trevor Gale, Lauren Gillespie, Karan Goel, Noah Goodman, Shelby Grossman, Neel Guha, Tatsunori Hashimoto, Peter Henderson, John Hewitt, Daniel E. Ho, Jenny Hong, Kyle Hsu, Jing Huang, Thomas Icard, Saahil Jain, Dan Jurafsky, Pratyusha Kalluri, Siddharth Karamcheti, Geoff Keeling, Fereshte Khani, Omar Khattab, Pang Wei Koh, Mark Krass, Ranjay Krishna, Rohith Kuditipudi, Ananya Kumar, Faisal Ladhak, Mina Lee, Tony Lee, Jure Leskovec, Isabelle Levent, Xiang Lisa Li, Xuechen Li, Tengyu Ma, Ali Malik, Christopher D. Manning, Suvir Mirchandani, Eric Mitchell, Zanele Munyikwa, Suraj Nair, Avanika Narayan, Deepak Narayanan, Ben Newman, Allen Nie, Juan Carlos Niebles, Hamed Nilforoshan, Julian Nyarko, Giray Ogut, Laurel Orr, Isabel Papadimitriou, Joon Sung Park, Chris Piech, Eva Portelance, Christopher Potts, Aditi Raghunathan, Rob Reich, Hongyu Ren, Frieda Rong, Yusuf Roohani, Camilo Ruiz, Jack Ryan, Christopher Ré, Dorsa Sadigh, Shiori Sagawa, Keshav Santhanam, Andy Shih, Krishnan Srinivasan, Alex Tamkin, Rohan Taori, Armin W. Thomas, Florian Tramèr, Rose E. Wang, William Wang, Bohan Wu, Jiajun Wu, Yuhuai Wu, Sang Michael Xie, Michihiro Yasunaga, Jiaxuan You, Matei Zaharia, Michael Zhang, Tianyi Zhang, Xikun Zhang, Yuhui Zhang, Lucia Zheng, Kaitlyn Zhou, and Percy Liang. 2022. On the opportunities and risks of foundation models. *Preprint*, arXiv:2108.07258.

Samuel R. Bowman, Gabor Angeli, Christopher Potts, and Christopher D. Manning. 2015. A large annotated corpus for learning natural language inference. In *Proceedings of the 2015 Conference on Empirical Methods in Natural Language Processing*, pages 632–642, Lisbon, Portugal. Association for Computational Linguistics.

Tom B. Brown, Benjamin Mann, Nick Ryder, Melanie Subbiah, Jared Kaplan, Prafulla Dhariwal, Arvind Neelakantan, Pranav Shyam, Girish Sastry, Amanda

Askell, Sandhini Agarwal, Ariel Herbert-Voss, Gretchen Krueger, Tom Henighan, Rewon Child, Aditya Ramesh, Daniel M. Ziegler, Jeffrey Wu, Clemens Winter, Christopher Hesse, Mark Chen, Eric Sigler, Mateusz Litwin, Scott Gray, Benjamin Chess, Jack Clark, Christopher Berner, Sam McCandlish, Alec Radford, Ilya Sutskever, and Dario Amodei. 2020. Language models are few-shot learners. *Preprint*, arXiv:2005.14165.

Zheng Cai, Maosong Cao, Haojiong Chen, Kai Chen, Keyu Chen, Xin Chen, Xun Chen, Zehui Chen, Zhi Chen, Pei Chu, Xiaoyi Dong, Haodong Duan, Qi Fan, Zhaoye Fei, Yang Gao, Jiaye Ge, Chenya Gu, Yuzhe Gu, Tao Gui, Aijia Guo, Qipeng Guo, Conghui He, Yingfan Hu, Ting Huang, Tao Jiang, Penglong Jiao, Zhenjiang Jin, Zhikai Lei, Jiaxing Li, Jingwen Li, Linyang Li, Shuaibin Li, Wei Li, Yining Li, Hongwei Liu, Jiangning Liu, Jiawei Hong, Kaiwen Liu, Kuikun Liu, Xiaoran Liu, Chengqi Lv, Haijun Lv, Kai Lv, Li Ma, Runyuan Ma, Zerun Ma, Wenchang Ning, Linke Ouyang, Jiantao Qiu, Yuan Qu, Fukai Shang, Yunfan Shao, Demin Song, Zifan Song, Zhihao Sui, Peng Sun, Yu Sun, Huanze Tang, Bin Wang, Guoteng Wang, Jiaqi Wang, Jiayu Wang, Rui Wang, Yudong Wang, Ziyi Wang, Xingjian Wei, Qizhen Weng, Fan Wu, Yingtong Xiong, Chao Xu, Ruiliang Xu, Hang Yan, Yirong Yan, Xiaogui Yang, Haochen Ye, Huaiyuan Ying, Jia Yu, Jing Yu, Yuhang Zang, Chuyu Zhang, Li Zhang, Pan Zhang, Peng Zhang, Ruijie Zhang, Shuo Zhang, Songyang Zhang, Wenjian Zhang, Wenwei Zhang, Xingcheng Zhang, Xinyue Zhang, Hui Zhao, Qian Zhao, Xiaomeng Zhao, Fengzhe Zhou, Zaida Zhou, Jingming Zhuo, Yicheng Zou, Xipeng Qiu, Yu Qiao, and Dahua Lin. 2024. Internlm2 technical report. *Preprint*, arXiv:2403.17297.

Oana-Maria Camburu, Tim Rocktäschel, Thomas Lukasiewicz, and Phil Blunsom. 2018. e-snli: Natural language inference with natural language explanations. *Preprint*, arXiv:1812.01193.

Mark Chen, Jerry Tworek, Heewoo Jun, Qiming Yuan, Henrique Ponde de Oliveira Pinto, Jared Kaplan, Harri Edwards, Yuri Burda, Nicholas Joseph, Greg Brockman, Alex Ray, Raul Puri, Gretchen Krueger, Michael Petrov, Heidy Khlaaf, Girish Sastry, Pamela Mishkin, Brooke Chan, Scott Gray, Nick Ryder, Mikhail Pavlov, Alethea Power, Lukasz Kaiser, Mohammad Bavarian, Clemens Winter, Philippe Tillet, Felipe Petroski Such, Dave Cummings, Matthias Plappert, Fotios Chantzis, Elizabeth Barnes, Ariel Herbert-Voss, William Hebgen Guss, Alex Nichol, Alex Paino, Nikolas Tezak, Jie Tang, Igor Babuschkin, Suchir Balaji, Shantanu Jain, William Saunders, Christopher Hesse, Andrew N. Carr, Jan Leike, Josh Achiam, Vedant Misra, Evan Morikawa, Alec Radford, Matthew Knight, Miles Brundage, Mira Murati, Katie Mayer, Peter Welinder, Bob McGrew, Dario Amodei, Sam McCandlish, Ilya Sutskever, and Wojciech Zaremba. 2021. Evaluating large language models trained on code.

Eunsol Choi, He He, Mohit Iyyer, Mark Yatskar, Wen tau Yih, Yejin Choi, Percy Liang, and Luke Zettlemoyer. 2018. Quac : Question answering in context. *Preprint*, arXiv:1808.07036.

Aakanksha Chowdhery, Sharan Narang, Jacob Devlin, Maarten Bosma, Gaurav Mishra, Adam Roberts, Paul Barham, Hyung Won Chung, Charles Sutton, Sebastian Gehrmann, Parker Schuh, Kensen Shi, Sasha Tsvyashchenko, Joshua Maynez, Abhishek Rao, Parker Barnes, Yi Tay, Noam Shazeer, Vinodkumar Prabhakaran, Emily Reif, Nan Du, Ben Hutchinson, Reiner Pope, James Bradbury, Jacob Austin, Michael Isard, Guy Gur-Ari, Pengcheng Yin, Toju Duke, Anselm Levskaya, Sanjay Ghemawat, Sunipa Dev, Henryk Michalewski, Xavier Garcia, Vedant Misra, Kevin Robinson, Liam Fedus, Denny Zhou, Daphne Ippolito, David Luan, Hyeontaek Lim, Barret Zoph, Alexander Spiridonov, Ryan Sepassi, David Dohan, Shivani Agrawal, Mark Omernick, Andrew M. Dai, Thanumalayan Sankaranarayana Pillai, Marie Pellat, Aitor Lewkowycz, Erica Moreira, Rewon Child, Oleksandr Polozov, Katherine Lee, Zongwei Zhou, Xuezhi Wang, Brennan Saeta, Mark Diaz, Orhan Firat, Michele Catasta, Jason Wei, Kathy Meier-Hellstern, Douglas Eck, Jeff Dean, Slav Petrov, and Noah Fiedel. 2022. Palm: Scaling language modeling with pathways. *Preprint*, arXiv:2204.02311.

Peter Clark, Isaac Cowhey, Oren Etzioni, Tushar Khot, Ashish Sabharwal, Carissa Schoenick, and Oyvind Tafjord. 2018. Think you have solved question answering? try arc, the ai2 reasoning challenge. *arXiv:1803.05457v1*.

Karl Cobbe, Vineet Kosaraju, Mohammad Bavarian, Mark Chen, Heewoo Jun, Lukasz Kaiser, Matthias Plappert, Jerry Tworek, Jacob Hilton, Reiichiro Nakano, Christopher Hesse, and John Schulman. 2021. Training verifiers to solve math word problems. *arXiv preprint arXiv:2110.14168*.

Arman Cohan, Waleed Ammar, Madeleine van Zuylen, and Field Cady. 2019. Structural scaffolds for citation intent classification in scientific publications. *Preprint*, arXiv:1904.01608.

Together Computer. 2023. Redpajama: an open dataset for training large language models.

Alexis Conneau, Ruty Rinott, Guillaume Lample, Adina Williams, Samuel R. Bowman, Holger Schwenk, and Veselin Stoyanov. 2018. Xnli: Evaluating cross-lingual sentence representations. In *Proceedings of the 2018 Conference on Empirical Methods in Natural Language Processing*. Association for Computational Linguistics.

Chunyuan Deng, Yilun Zhao, Xiangru Tang, Mark Gerstein, and Arman Cohan. 2024. Investigating data contamination in modern benchmarks for large language models. In *Proceedings of the 2024 Conference of the North American Chapter of the Association for Computational Linguistics: Human Language Technologies (Volume 1: Long Papers)*, pages 8698–8711, Mexico City, Mexico. Association for Computational Linguistics.

Jesse Dodge, Maarten Sap, Ana Marasović, William Agnew, Gabriel Ilharco, Dirk Groeneveld, Margaret Mitchell, and Matt Gardner. 2021. Documenting large webtext corpora: A case study on the colossal clean crawled corpus. In *Proceedings of the 2021 Conference on Empirical Methods in Natural Language Processing*, pages 1286–1305, Online and Punta Cana, Dominican Republic. Association for Computational Linguistics.

Yihong Dong, Xue Jiang, Huanyu Liu, Zhi Jin, Bin Gu, Mengfei Yang, and Ge Li. 2024. Generalization or memorization: Data contamination and trustworthy evaluation for large language models. *Preprint*, arXiv:2402.15938.

Nan Du, Yanping Huang, Andrew M. Dai, Simon Tong, Dmitry Lepikhin, Yuanzhong Xu, Maxim Krikun, Yanqi Zhou, Adams Wei Yu, Orhan Firat, Barret Zoph, Liam Fedus, Maarten Bosma, Zongwei Zhou, Tao Wang, Yu Emma Wang, Kellie Webster, Marie Pellat, Kevin Robinson, Kathleen Meier-Hellstern, Toju Duke, Lucas Dixon, Kun Zhang, Quoc V Le, Yonghui Wu, Zhifeng Chen, and Claire Cui. 2022a. Glam: Efficient scaling of language models with mixture-of-experts. *Preprint*, arXiv:2112.06905.

Zhengxiao Du, Yujie Qian, Xiao Liu, Ming Ding, Jiezhong Qiu, Zhilin Yang, and Jie Tang. 2022b. Glm: General language model pretraining with autoregressive blank infilling. In *Proceedings of the 60th Annual Meeting of the Association for Computational Linguistics (Volume 1: Long Papers)*, pages 320–335.

Dheeru Dua, Yizhong Wang, Pradeep Dasigi, Gabriel Stanovsky, Sameer Singh, and Matt Gardner. 2019. DROP: A reading comprehension benchmark requiring discrete reasoning over paragraphs. In *Proc. of NAACL*.

Yanai Elazar, Akshita Bhagia, Ian Helgi Magnusson, Abhilasha Ravichander, Dustin Schwenk, Alane Suhr, Evan Pete Walsh, Dirk Groeneveld, Luca Soldaini, Sameer Singh, Hannaneh Hajishirzi, Noah A. Smith, and Jesse Dodge. 2024. What's in my big data? In *The Twelfth International Conference on Learning Representations*.

Maxim Enis and Mark Hopkins. 2024. From llm to nmt: Advancing low-resource machine translation with claude. *Preprint*, arXiv:2404.13813.

Leo Gao, Stella Biderman, Sid Black, Laurence Golding, Travis Hoppe, Charles Foster, Jason Phang, Horace He, Anish Thite, Noa Nabeshima, Shawn Presser, and Connor Leahy. 2020. The pile: An 800gb dataset of diverse text for language modeling. *Preprint*, arXiv:2101.00027.

Bogdan Gliwa, Iwona Mochol, Maciej Biesek, and Aleksander Wawer. 2019. Samsum corpus: A human-annotated dialogue dataset for abstractive summarization. *arXiv preprint arXiv:1911.12237*.

Shahriar Golchin and Mihai Surdeanu. 2024a. Data contamination quiz: A tool to detect and estimate contamination in large language models. *Preprint*, arXiv:2311.06233.

Shahriar Golchin and Mihai Surdeanu. 2024b. Time travel in LLMs: Tracing data contamination in large language models. In *The Twelfth International Conference on Learning Representations*.

David Graff, Junbo Kong, Ke Chen, and Kazuaki Maeda. 2003. English gigaword. *Linguistic Data Consortium, Philadelphia*, 4(1):34.

Tahmid Hasan, Abhik Bhattacharjee, Md. Saiful Islam, Kazi Mubasshir, Yuan-Fang Li, Yong-Bin Kang, M. Sohel Rahman, and Rifat Shahriyar. 2021. XL-sum: Large-scale multilingual abstractive summarization for 44 languages. In *Findings of the Association for Computational Linguistics: ACL-IJCNLP 2021*, pages 4693–4703, Online. Association for Computational Linguistics.

Dan Hendrycks, Collin Burns, Steven Basart, Andy Zou, Mantas Mazeika, Dawn Song, and Jacob Steinhardt. 2021a. Measuring massive multitask language understanding. *Proceedings of the International Conference on Learning Representations (ICLR)*.

Dan Hendrycks, Collin Burns, Saurav Kadavath, Akul Arora, Steven Basart, Eric Tang, Dawn Song, and Jacob Steinhardt. 2021b. Measuring mathematical problem solving with the math dataset. *NeurIPS*.

Yuzhen Huang, Yuzhuo Bai, Zhihao Zhu, Junlei Zhang, Jinghan Zhang, Tangjun Su, Junteng Liu, Chuancheng Lv, Yikai Zhang, Jiayi Lei, Yao Fu, Maosong Sun, and Junxian He. 2023. C-eval: A multi-level multi-discipline chinese evaluation suite for foundation models. *arXiv preprint arXiv:2305.08322*.

Dieuwke Hupkes, Mario Giulianelli, Verna Dankers, Mikel Artetxe, Yanai Elazar, Tiago Pimentel, Christos Christodoulopoulos, Karim Lasri, Naomi Saphra, Arabella Sinclair, Dennis Ulmer, Florian Schottmann, Khuyagbaatar Batsuren, Kaiser Sun, Koustuv Sinha, Leila Khalatbari, Maria Ryskina, Rita Frieske, Ryan Cotterell, and Zhijing Jin. 2023. A taxonomy and review of generalization research in nlp. *Nature Machine Intelligence*, 5(10):1161–1174.

Alon Jacovi, Avi Caciularu, Omer Goldman, and Yoav Goldberg. 2023. Stop uploading test data in plain text: Practical strategies for mitigating data contamination by evaluation benchmarks. In *Proceedings of the 2023 Conference on Empirical Methods in Natural Language Processing*, pages 5075–5084, Singapore. Association for Computational Linguistics.

Tim Jansen, Yangling Tong, Victoria Zevallos, and Pedro Ortiz Suarez. 2022. Perplexed by Quality: A Perplexity-based Method for Adult and Harmful Content Detection in Multilingual Heterogeneous Web Data. *arXiv e-prints*, arXiv:2212.10440.

Albert Q. Jiang, Alexandre Sablayrolles, Arthur Mensch, Chris Bamford, Devendra Singh Chaplot, Diego de las Casas, Florian Bressand, Gianna Lengyel, Guillaume Lample, Lucile Saulnier, Lélio Renard Lavaud, Marie-Anne Lachaux, Pierre Stock, Teven Le Scao, Thibaut Lavril, Thomas Wang, Timothée Lacroix, and William El Sayed. 2023. Mistral 7b. *Preprint*, arXiv:2310.06825.

Mandar Joshi, Eunsol Choi, Daniel Weld, and Luke Zettlemoyer. 2017. TriviaQA: A large scale distantly supervised challenge dataset for reading comprehension. In *Proceedings of the 55th Annual Meeting of the Association for Computational Linguistics (Volume 1: Long Papers)*, pages 1601–1611, Vancouver, Canada. Association for Computational Linguistics.

Phillip Keung, Yichao Lu, György Szarvas, and Noah A. Smith. 2020. The multilingual amazon reviews corpus. In *Proceedings of the 2020 Conference on Empirical Methods in Natural Language Processing*.

Tushar Khot, Ashish Sabharwal, and Peter Clark. 2018. SciTail: A textual entailment dataset from science question answering. In *AAAI*.

Byeongchang Kim, Hyunwoo Kim, and Gunhee Kim. 2018. Abstractive summarization of reddit posts with multi-level memory networks. *Preprint*, arXiv:1811.00783.

Denis Kocetkov, Raymond Li, Loubna Ben Allal, Jia Li, Chenghao Mou, Carlos Muñoz Ferrandis, Yacine Jernite, Margaret Mitchell, Sean Hughes, Thomas Wolf, Dzmitry Bahdanau, Leandro von Werra, and Harm de Vries. 2022. The stack: 3 tb of permissively licensed source code. *Preprint*.

Anastassia Kornilova and Vlad Eidelman. 2019. Billsum: A corpus for automatic summarization of us legislation. *arXiv preprint arXiv:1910.00523*.

Neema Kotonya and Francesca Toni. 2020. Explainable automated fact-checking for public health claims. In *Proceedings of the 2020 Conference on Empirical Methods in Natural Language Processing (EMNLP)*, pages 7740–7754, Online. Association for Computational Linguistics.

Julia Kreutzer, Isaac Caswell, Lisa Wang, Ahsan Wahab, Daan van Esch, Nasanbayar Ulzii-Orshikh, Allahsera Tapo, Nishant Subramani, Artem Sokolov, Claytone Sikasote, Monang Setyawan, Supheakmungkol Sarin, Sokhar Samb, Benoît Sagot, Clara Rivera, Annette Rios, Isabel Papadimitriou, Salomey Osei, Pedro Ortiz Suarez, Iroro Orife, Kelechi Ogueji, Andre Niyongabo Rubungo, Toan Q. Nguyen, Mathias Müller, André Müller, Shamsuddeen Hassan Muhammad, Nanda Muhammad, Ayanda Mnyakeni, Jamshidbek Mirzakhalov, Tapiwanashe Matangira, Colin Leong, Nze Lawson, Sneha Kudugunta, Yacine Jernite, Mathias Jenny, Orhan Firat, Bonaventure F. P. Dossou, Sakhile Dlamini, Nisansa de Silva, Sakine Çabuk Ballı, Stella Biderman, Alessia Battisti, Ahmed Baruwa, Ankur Bapna, Pallavi Baljekar, Israel Abebe Azime, Ayodele Awokoya, Duygu Ataman, Orevaoghene Ahia, Oghenefego Ahia, Sweta Agrawal, and Mofetoluwa Adeyemi. 2022. Quality at a glance: An audit of web-crawled multilingual datasets. *Transactions of the Association for Computational Linguistics*, 10:50–72.

Tom Kwiatkowski, Jennimaria Palomaki, Olivia Redfield, Michael Collins, Ankur Parikh, Chris Alberti, Danielle Epstein, Illia Polosukhin, Matthew Kelcey, Jacob Devlin, Kenton Lee, Kristina N. Toutanova, Llion Jones, Ming-Wei Chang, Andrew Dai, Jakob Uszkoreit, Quoc Le, and Slav Petrov. 2019. Natural questions: a benchmark for question answering research. *Transactions of the Association of Computational Linguistics*.

Faisal Ladhak, Esin Durmus, Claire Cardie, and Kathleen McKeown. 2020. WikiLingua: A new benchmark dataset for cross-lingual abstractive summarization. In *Findings of the Association for Computational Linguistics: EMNLP 2020*, pages 4034–4048, Online. Association for Computational Linguistics.

Rémi Lebret, David Grangier, and Michael Auli. 2016. Generating text from structured data with application to the biography domain. *CoRR*, abs/1603.07771.

Hector Levesque, Ernest Davis, and Leora Morgenstern. 2012. The winograd schema challenge. In *Thirteenth International Conference on the Principles of Knowledge Representation and Reasoning*. Citeseer.

Yucheng Li, Frank Guerin, and Chenghua Lin. 2024. An open source data contamination report for large language models. *Preprint*, arXiv:2310.17589.

Stephanie Lin, Jacob Hilton, and Owain Evans. 2022. Truthfulqa: Measuring how models mimic human falsehoods. *Preprint*, arXiv:2109.07958.

Andrew L. Maas, Raymond E. Daly, Peter T. Pham, Dan Huang, Andrew Y. Ng, and Christopher Potts. 2011. Learning word vectors for sentiment analysis. In *Proceedings of the 49th Annual Meeting of the Association for Computational Linguistics: Human Language Technologies*, pages 142–150, Portland, Oregon, USA. Association for Computational Linguistics.

Inbal Magar and Roy Schwartz. 2022. Data contamination: From memorization to exploitation. In *Proceedings of the 60th Annual Meeting of the Association for Computational Linguistics (Volume 2: Short Papers)*, pages 157–165, Dublin, Ireland. Association for Computational Linguistics.

Ian Magnusson, Akshita Bhagia, Valentin Hofmann, Luca Soldaini, A. Jha, Oyvind Tafjord, Dustin Schwenk, Evan Pete Walsh, Yanai Elazar, Kyle Lo, Dirk Groeneveld, Iz Beltagy, Hannaneh Hajishirzi, Noah A. Smith, Kyle Richardson, and Jesse Dodge. 2023. Paloma: A benchmark for evaluating language model fit. *arXiv preprint arXiv:2312.10523*.

Marco Marelli, Luisa Bentivogli, Marco Baroni, Raffaella Bernardi, Stefano Menini, and Roberto Zamparelli. 2014. Semeval-2014 task 1: Evaluation of compositional distributional semantic models on full sentences through semantic relatedness and textual entailment.

Philip May. 2021. Machine translated multilingual sts benchmark dataset.

William Merrill, Noah A. Smith, and Yanai Elazar. 2024. Evaluating n-gram novelty of language models using rusty-dawg. *arXiv preprint arXiv:2406.13069*.

Todor Mihaylov, Peter Clark, Tushar Khot, and Ashish Sabharwal. 2018. Can a suit of armor conduct electricity? a new dataset for open book question answering. In *Conference on Empirical Methods in Natural Language Processing*.

John Miller, Karl Krauth, Benjamin Recht, and Ludwig Schmidt. 2020. The effect of natural distribution shift on question answering models. In *Proceedings of the 37th International Conference on Machine Learning*, volume 119 of *Proceedings of Machine Learning Research*, pages 6905–6916. PMLR.

Margaret Mitchell, Alexandra Sasha Luccioni, Nathan Lambert, Marissa Gerchick, Angelina McMillan-Major, Ezinwanne Ozoani, Nazneen Rajani, Tristan Thrush, Yacine Jernite, and Douwe Kiela. 2023. Measuring data. *Preprint*, arXiv:2212.05129.

Niklas Muennighoff, Thomas Wang, Lintang Sutawika, Adam Roberts, Stella Biderman, Teven Le Scao, M Saiful Bari, Sheng Shen, Zheng Xin Yong, Hailey Schoelkopf, Xiangru Tang, Dragomir Radev, Alham Fikri Aji, Khalid Almubarak, Samuel Albanie, Zaid Alyafeai, Albert Webson, Edward Raff, and Colin Raffel. 2023. Crosslingual generalization through multitask finetuning. In *Proceedings of the 61st Annual Meeting of the Association for Computational Linguistics (Volume 1: Long Papers)*, pages 15991–16111, Toronto, Canada. Association for Computational Linguistics.

Niklas Muennighoff, Thomas Wang, Lintang Sutawika, Adam Roberts, Stella Biderman, Teven Le Scao, M Saiful Bari, Sheng Shen, Zheng-Xin Yong, Hailey Schoelkopf, et al. 2022. Crosslingual generalization through multitask finetuning. *arXiv preprint arXiv:2211.01786*.

Nikita Nangia, Clara Vania, Rasika Bhalerao, and Samuel R. Bowman. 2020. CrowS-Pairs: A Challenge Dataset for Measuring Social Biases in Masked Language Models. In *Proceedings of the 2020 Conference on Empirical Methods in Natural Language Processing*, Online. Association for Computational Linguistics.

Shashi Narayan, Shay B. Cohen, and Mirella Lapata. 2018. Don't give me the details, just the summary! topic-aware convolutional neural networks for extreme summarization. *ArXiv*, abs/1808.08745.

Yixin Nie, Adina Williams, Emily Dinan, Mohit Bansal, Jason Weston, and Douwe Kiela. 2020. Adversarial NLI: A new benchmark for natural language understanding. In *Proceedings of the 58th Annual Meeting of the Association for Computational Linguistics*. Association for Computational Linguistics.

NLLB-Team, Marta R. Costa-jussà, James Cross, Onur Çelebi, Maha Elbayad, Kenneth Heafield, Kevin Heffernan, Elahe Kalbassi, Janice Lam, Daniel Licht, Jean Maillard, Anna Sun, Skyler Wang, Guillaume Wenzek, Al Youngblood, Bapi Akula, Loic Barrault, Gabriel Mejia Gonzalez, Prangthip Hansanti, John Hoffman, Semarley Jarrett, Kaushik Ram Sadagopan, Dirk Rowe, Shannon Spruit, Chau Tran, Pierre Andrews, Necip Fazil Ayan, Shruti Bhosale, Sergey Edunov, Angela Fan, Cynthia Gao, Vedanuj Goswami, Francisco Guzmán, Philipp Koehn, Alexandre Mourachko, Christophe Ropers, Safiyyah Saleem, Holger Schwenk, and Jeff Wang. 2022. No language left behind: Scaling human-centered machine translation.

OpenAI, Josh Achiam, Steven Adler, Sandhini Agarwal, Lama Ahmad, Ilge Akkaya, Florencia Leoni Aleman, Diogo Almeida, Janko Altenschmidt, Sam Altman, Shyamal Anadkat, Red Avila, Igor Babuschkin, Suchir Balaji, Valerie Balcom, Paul Baltescu, Haiming Bao, Mohammad Bavarian, Jeff Belgum, Irwan Bello, Jake Berdine, Gabriel Bernadett-Shapiro, Christopher Berner, Lenny Bogdonoff, Oleg Boiko, Madelaine Boyd, Anna-Luisa Brakman, Greg Brockman, Tim Brooks, Miles Brundage, Kevin Button, Trevor Cai, Rosie Campbell, Andrew Cann, Brittany Carey, Chelsea Carlson, Rory Carmichael, Brooke Chan, Che Chang, Fotis Chantzis, Derek Chen, Sully Chen, Ruby Chen, Jason Chen, Mark Chen, Ben Chess, Chester Cho, Casey Chu, Hyung Won Chung, Dave Cummings, Jeremiah Currier, Yunxing Dai, Cory Decareaux, Thomas Degry, Noah Deutsch, Damien Deville, Arka Dhar, David Dohan, Steve Dowling, Sheila Dunning, Adrien Ecoffet, Atty Eleti, Tyna Eloundou, David Farhi, Liam Fedus, Niko Felix, Simón Posada Fishman, Juston Forte, Isabella Fulford, Leo Gao, Elie Georges, Christian Gibson, Vik Goel, Tarun Gogineni, Gabriel Goh, Rapha Gontijo-Lopes, Jonathan Gordon, Morgan Grafstein, Scott Gray, Ryan Greene, Joshua Gross, Shixiang Shane Gu, Yufei Guo, Chris Hallacy, Jesse Han, Jeff Harris, Yuchen He, Mike Heaton, Johannes Heidecke, Chris Hesse, Alan Hickey, Wade Hickey, Peter Hoeschele, Brandon Houghton, Kenny Hsu, Shengli Hu, Xin Hu, Joost Huizinga, Shantanu Jain, Shawn Jain, Joanne Jang, Angela Jiang, Roger Jiang, Haozhun Jin, Denny Jin, Shino Jomoto, Billie Jonn, Heewoo Jun, Tomer Kaftan, Łukasz Kaiser, Ali Kamali, Ingmar Kanitscheider, Nitish Shirish Keskar, Tabarak Khan, Logan Kilpatrick, Jong Wook Kim, Christina Kim, Yongjik Kim, Jan Hendrik Kirchner, Jamie Kiros, Matt Knight, Daniel Kokotajlo, Łukasz Kondraciuk, Andrew Kondrich, Aris Konstantinidis, Kyle Kosic, Gretchen Krueger, Vishal Kuo, Michael Lampe, Ikai Lan, Teddy Lee, Jan Leike, Jade Leung, Daniel Levy, Chak Ming Li,

Rachel Lim, Molly Lin, Stephanie Lin, Mateusz Litwin, Theresa Lopez, Ryan Lowe, Patricia Lue, Anna Makanju, Kim Malfacini, Sam Manning, Todor Markov, Yaniv Markovski, Bianca Martin, Katie Mayer, Andrew Mayne, Bob McGrew, Scott Mayer McKinney, Christine McLeavey, Paul McMillan, Jake McNeil, David Medina, Aalok Mehta, Jacob Menick, Luke Metz, Andrey Mishchenko, Pamela Mishkin, Vinnie Monaco, Evan Morikawa, Daniel Mossing, Tong Mu, Mira Murati, Oleg Murk, David Mély, Ashvin Nair, Reiichiro Nakano, Rajeev Nayak, Arvind Neelakantan, Richard Ngo, Hyeonwoo Noh, Long Ouyang, Cullen O'Keefe, Jakub Pachocki, Alex Paino, Joe Palermo, Ashley Pantuliano, Giambattista Parascandolo, Joel Parish, Emy Parparita, Alex Passos, Mikhail Pavlov, Andrew Peng, Adam Perelman, Filipe de Avila Belbute Peres, Michael Petrov, Henrique Ponde de Oliveira Pinto, Michael, Pokorny, Michelle Pokrass, Vitchyr H. Pong, Tolly Powell, Alethea Power, Boris Power, Elizabeth Proehl, Raul Puri, Alec Radford, Jack Rae, Aditya Ramesh, Cameron Raymond, Francis Real, Kendra Rimbach, Carl Ross, Bob Rotsted, Henri Roussez, Nick Ryder, Mario Saltarelli, Ted Sanders, Shibani Santurkar, Girish Sastry, Heather Schmidt, David Schnurr, John Schulman, Daniel Selsam, Kyla Sheppard, Toki Sherbakov, Jessica Shieh, Sarah Shoker, Pranav Shyam, Szymon Sidor, Eric Sigler, Maddie Simens, Jordan Sitkin, Katarina Slama, Ian Sohl, Benjamin Sokolowsky, Yang Song, Natalie Staudacher, Felipe Petroski Such, Natalie Summers, Ilya Sutskever, Jie Tang, Nikolas Tezak, Madeleine B. Thompson, Phil Tillet, Amin Tootoonchian, Elizabeth Tseng, Preston Tuggle, Nick Turley, Jerry Tworek, Juan Felipe Cerón Uribe, Andrea Vallone, Arun Vijayvergiya, Chelsea Voss, Carroll Wainwright, Justin Jay Wang, Alvin Wang, Ben Wang, Jonathan Ward, Jason Wei, CJ Weinmann, Akila Welihinda, Peter Welinder, Jiayi Weng, Lilian Weng, Matt Wiethoff, Dave Willner, Clemens Winter, Samuel Wolrich, Hannah Wong, Lauren Workman, Sherwin Wu, Jeff Wu, Michael Wu, Kai Xiao, Tao Xu, Sarah Yoo, Kevin Yu, Qiming Yuan, Wojciech Zaremba, Rowan Zellers, Chong Zhang, Marvin Zhang, Shengjia Zhao, Tianhao Zheng, Juntang Zhuang, William Zhuk, and Barret Zoph. 2024. Gpt-4 technical report. *Preprint*, arXiv:2303.08774.

Yonatan Oren, Nicole Meister, Niladri S. Chatterji, Faisal Ladhak, and Tatsunori Hashimoto. 2024. Proving test set contamination in black-box language models. In *The Twelfth International Conference on Learning Representations*.

Pedro Javier Ortiz Su'arez, Laurent Romary, and Benoit Sagot. 2020. A monolingual approach to contextualized word embeddings for mid-resource languages. In *Proceedings of the 58th Annual Meeting of the Association for Computational Linguistics*, pages 1703–1714, Online. Association for Computational Linguistics.

Pedro Javier Ortiz Su'arez, Benoit Sagot, and Laurent Romary. 2019. Asynchronous pipelines for processing huge corpora on medium to low resource infrastructures. Proceedings of the Workshop on Challenges in the Management of Large Corpora (CMLC-7) 2019. Cardiff, 22nd July 2019, pages 9 – 16, Mannheim. Leibniz-Institut f"ur Deutsche Sprache.

Denis Paperno, Germán Kruszewski, Angeliki Lazaridou, Ngoc Quan Pham, Raffaella Bernardi, Sandro Pezzelle, Marco Baroni, Gemma Boleda, and Raquel Fernandez. 2016. The LAMBADA dataset: Word prediction requiring a broad discourse context. In *Proceedings of the 54th Annual Meeting of the Association for Computational Linguistics (Volume 1: Long Papers)*, pages 1525–1534, Berlin, Germany. Association for Computational Linguistics.

F. Petroni, T. Rocktäschel, A. H. Miller, P. Lewis, A. Bakhtin, Y. Wu, and S. Riedel. 2019. Language models as knowledge bases? In *Proceedings of the 2019 Conference on Empirical Methods in Natural Language Processing (EMNLP)*.

Fabio Petroni, Patrick Lewis, Aleksandra Piktus, Tim Rocktäschel, Yuxiang Wu, Alexander H. Miller, and Sebastian Riedel. 2020. How context affects language models' factual predictions. In *Automated Knowledge Base Construction*.

Colin Raffel, Noam Shazeer, Adam Roberts, Katherine Lee, Sharan Narang, Michael Matena, Yanqi Zhou, Wei Li, and Peter J. Liu. 2023. Exploring the limits of transfer learning with a unified text-to-text transformer. *Preprint*, arXiv:1910.10683.

Pranav Rajpurkar, Robin Jia, and Percy Liang. 2018. Know what you don't know: Unanswerable questions for SQuAD. In *Proceedings of the 56th Annual Meeting of the Association for Computational Linguistics (Volume 2: Short Papers)*, pages 784–789, Melbourne, Australia. Association for Computational Linguistics.

Pranav Rajpurkar, Jian Zhang, Konstantin Lopyrev, and Percy Liang. 2016. SQuAD: 100,000+ questions for machine comprehension of text. In *Proceedings of the 2016 Conference on Empirical Methods in Natural Language Processing*, pages 2383–2392, Austin, Texas. Association for Computational Linguistics.

Ahad Rana. 2010. Common crawl – building an open web-scale crawl using hadoop.

Federico Ranaldi, Elena Sofia Ruzzetti, Dario Onorati, Leonardo Ranaldi, Cristina Giannone, Andrea Favalli, Raniero Romagnoli, and Fabio Massimo Zanzotto. 2024. Investigating the impact of data contamination of large language models in text-to-sql translation. *Preprint*, arXiv:2402.08100.

Siva Reddy, Danqi Chen, and Christopher D. Manning. 2019. CoQA: A conversational question answering challenge. *Transactions of the Association for Computational Linguistics*, 7:249–266.

Martin Riddell, Ansong Ni, and Arman Cohan. 2024. Quantifying contamination in evaluating code generation capabilities of language models. *Preprint*, arXiv:2403.04811.

Amrita Saha, Rahul Aralikatte, Mitesh M. Khapra, and Karthik Sankaranarayanan. 2018. DuoRC: Towards Complex Language Understanding with Paraphrased Reading Comprehension. In *Meeting of the Association for Computational Linguistics (ACL)*.

Oscar Sainz, Jon Campos, Iker García-Ferrero, Julen Etxaniz, Oier Lopez de Lacalle, and Eneko Agirre. 2023a. NLP evaluation in trouble: On the need to measure LLM data contamination for each benchmark. In *Findings of the Association for Computational Linguistics: EMNLP 2023*, pages 10776–10787, Singapore. Association for Computational Linguistics.

Oscar Sainz, Jon Ander Campos, Iker García-Ferrero, Julen Etxaniz, and Eneko Agirre. 2023b. Did chatgpt cheat on your test?

Rishi Sharma, James Allen, Omid Bakhshandeh, and Nasrin Mostafazadeh. 2018. Tackling the story ending biases in the story cloze test. In *Proceedings of the 56th Annual Meeting of the Association for Computational Linguistics (Volume 2: Short Papers)*, pages 752–757, Melbourne, Australia. Association for Computational Linguistics.

Emily Silcock, Luca D'Amico-Wong, Jinglin Yang, and Melissa Dell. 2023. Noise-robust de-duplication at scale. In *The Eleventh International Conference on Learning Representations*.

Aarohi Srivastava, Abhinav Rastogi, Abhishek Rao, Abu Awal Md Shoeb, Abubakar Abid, Adam Fisch, Adam R. Brown, Adam Santoro, Aditya Gupta, Adrià Garriga-Alonso, Agnieszka Kluska, Aitor Lewkowycz, Akshat Agarwal, Alethea Power, Alex Ray, Alex Warstadt, Alexander W. Kocurek, Ali Safaya, Ali Tazarv, Alice Xiang, Alicia Parrish, Allen Nie, Aman Hussain, Amanda Askell, Amanda Dsouza, Ambrose Slone, Ameet Rahane, Anantharaman S. Iyer, Anders Andreassen, Andrea Madotto, Andrea Santilli, Andreas Stuhlmüller, Andrew Dai, Andrew La, Andrew Lampinen, Andy Zou, Angela Jiang, Angelica Chen, Anh Vuong, Animesh Gupta, Anna Gottardi, Antonio Norelli, Anu Venkatesh, Arash Gholamidavoodi, Arfa Tabassum, Arul Menezes, Arun Kirubarajan, Asher Mullokandov, Ashish Sabharwal, Austin Herrick, Avia Efrat, Aykut Erdem, Ayla Karakaş, B. Ryan Roberts, Bao Sheng Loe, Barret Zoph, Bartłomiej Bojanowski, Batuhan Özyurt, Behnam Hedayatnia, Behnam Neyshabur, Benjamin Inden, Benno Stein, Berk Ekmekci, Bill Yuchen Lin, Blake Howald, Bryan Orinion, Cameron Diao, Cameron Dour, Catherine Stinson, Cedrick Argueta, César Ferri Ramírez, Chandan Singh, Charles Rathkopf, Chenlin Meng, Chitta Baral, Chiyu Wu, Chris Callison-Burch, Chris Waites, Christian Voigt, Christopher D. Manning, Christopher Potts, Cindy Ramirez, Clara E. Rivera, Clemencia Siro, Colin Raffel, Courtney Ashcraft, Cristina Garbacea, Damien Sileo, Dan Garrette, Dan Hendrycks, Dan Kilman, Dan Roth, Daniel Freeman, Daniel Khashabi, Daniel Levy, Daniel Moseguí González, Danielle Perszyk, Danny Hernandez, Danqi Chen, Daphne Ippolito, Dar Gilboa, David Dohan, David Drakard, David Jurgens, Debajyoti Datta, Deep Ganguli, Denis Emelin, Denis Kleyko, Deniz Yuret, Derek Chen, Derek Tam, Dieuwke Hupkes, Diganta Misra, Dilyar Buzan, Dimitri Coelho Mollo, Diyi Yang, Dong-Ho Lee, Dylan Schrader, Ekaterina Shutova, Ekin Dogus Cubuk, Elad Segal, Eleanor Hagerman, Elizabeth Barnes, Elizabeth Donoway, Ellie Pavlick, Emanuele Rodola, Emma Lam, Eric Chu, Eric Tang, Erkut Erdem, Ernie Chang, Ethan A. Chi, Ethan Dyer, Ethan Jerzak, Ethan Kim, Eunice Engefu Manyasi, Evgenii Zheltonozhskii, Fanyue Xia, Fatemeh Siar, Fernando Martínez-Plumed, Francesca Happé, Francois Chollet, Frieda Rong, Gaurav Mishra, Genta Indra Winata, Gerard de Melo, Germán Kruszewski, Giambattista Parascandolo, Giorgio Mariani, Gloria Wang, Gonzalo Jaimovitch-López, Gregor Betz, Guy Gur-Ari, Hana Galijasevic, Hannah Kim, Hannah Rashkin, Hannaneh Hajishirzi, Harsh Mehta, Hayden Bogar, Henry Shevlin, Hinrich Schütze, Hiromu Yakura, Hongming Zhang, Hugh Mee Wong, Ian Ng, Isaac Noble, Jaap Jumelet, Jack Geissinger, Jackson Kernion, Jacob Hilton, Jaehoon Lee, Jaime Fernández Fisac, James B. Simon, James Koppel, James Zheng, James Zou, Jan Kocoń, Jana Thompson, Janelle Wingfield, Jared Kaplan, Jarema Radom, Jascha Sohl-Dickstein, Jason Phang, Jason Wei, Jason Yosinski, Jekaterina Novikova, Jelle Bosscher, Jennifer Marsh, Jeremy Kim, Jeroen Taal, Jesse Engel, Jesujoba Alabi, Jiacheng Xu, Jiaming Song, Jillian Tang, Joan Waweru, John Burden, John Miller, John U. Balis, Jonathan Batchelder, Jonathan Berant, Jörg Frohberg, Jos Rozen, Jose Hernandez-Orallo, Joseph Boudeman, Joseph Guerr, Joseph Jones, Joshua B. Tenenbaum, Joshua S. Rule, Joyce Chua, Kamil Kanclerz, Karen Livescu, Karl Krauth, Karthik Gopalakrishnan, Katerina Ignatyeva, Katja Markert, Kaustubh D. Dhole, Kevin Gimpel, Kevin Omondi, Kory Mathewson, Kristen Chiafullo, Ksenia Shkaruta, Kumar Shridhar, Kyle McDonell, Kyle Richardson, Laria Reynolds, Leo Gao, Li Zhang, Liam Dugan, Lianhui Qin, Lidia Contreras-Ochando, Louis-Philippe Morency, Luca Moschella, Lucas Lam, Lucy Noble, Ludwig Schmidt, Luheng He, Luis Oliveros Colón, Luke Metz, Lütfi Kerem Şenel, Maarten Bosma, Maarten Sap, Maartje ter Hoeve, Maheen Farooqi, Manaal Faruqui, Mantas Mazeika, Marco Baturan, Marco Marelli, Marco Maru, Maria Jose Ramírez Quintana, Marie Tolkiehn, Mario Giulianelli, Martha Lewis, Martin Potthast, Matthew L. Leavitt, Matthias Hagen, Mátyás Schubert, Medina Orduna Baitemirova, Melody Arnaud, Melvin McElrath, Michael A. Yee, Michael Cohen, Michael Gu, Michael Ivanitskiy, Michael Starritt, Michael Strube, Michał Swędrowski, Michele Bevilacqua, Michihiro Yasunaga, Mihir Kale, Mike Cain, Mimee Xu, Mirac Suzgun, Mitch Walker, Mo Tiwari, Mohit Bansal, Moin Aminnaseri, Mor Geva, Mozhdeh Gheini, Mukund Varma T, Nanyun

Peng, Nathan A. Chi, Nayeon Lee, Neta Gur-Ari Krakover, Nicholas Cameron, Nicholas Roberts, Nick Doiron, Nicole Martinez, Nikita Nangia, Niklas Deckers, Niklas Muennighoff, Nitish Shirish Keskar, Niveditha S. Iyer, Noah Constant, Noah Fiedel, Nuan Wen, Oliver Zhang, Omar Agha, Omar Elbaghdadi, Omer Levy, Owain Evans, Pablo Antonio Moreno Casares, Parth Doshi, Pascale Fung, Paul Pu Liang, Paul Vicol, Pegah Alipoormolabashi, Peiyuan Liao, Percy Liang, Peter Chang, Peter Eckersley, Phu Mon Htut, Pinyu Hwang, Piotr Miłkowski, Piyush Patil, Pouya Pezeshkpour, Priti Oli, Qiaozhu Mei, Qing Lyu, Qinlang Chen, Rabin Banjade, Rachel Etta Rudolph, Raefer Gabriel, Rahel Habacker, Ramon Risco, Raphaël Millière, Rhythm Garg, Richard Barnes, Rif A. Saurous, Riku Arakawa, Robbe Raymaekers, Robert Frank, Rohan Sikand, Roman Novak, Roman Sitelew, Ronan LeBras, Rosanne Liu, Rowan Jacobs, Rui Zhang, Ruslan Salakhutdinov, Ryan Chi, Ryan Lee, Ryan Stovall, Ryan Teehan, Rylan Yang, Sahib Singh, Saif M. Mohammad, Sajant Anand, Sam Dillavou, Sam Shleifer, Sam Wiseman, Samuel Gruetter, Samuel R. Bowman, Samuel S. Schoenholz, Sanghyun Han, Sanjeev Kwatra, Sarah A. Rous, Sarik Ghazarian, Sayan Ghosh, Sean Casey, Sebastian Bischoff, Sebastian Gehrmann, Sebastian Schuster, Sepideh Sadeghi, Shadi Hamdan, Sharon Zhou, Shashank Srivastava, Sherry Shi, Shikhar Singh, Shima Asaadi, Shixiang Shane Gu, Shubh Pachchigar, Shubham Toshniwal, Shyam Upadhyay, Shyamolima, Debnath, Siamak Shakeri, Simon Thormeyer, Simone Melzi, Siva Reddy, Sneha Priscilla Makini, Soo-Hwan Lee, Spencer Torene, Sriharsha Hatwar, Stanislas Dehaene, Stefan Divic, Stefano Ermon, Stella Biderman, Stephanie Lin, Stephen Prasad, Steven T. Piantadosi, Stuart M. Shieber, Summer Misherghi, Svetlana Kiritchenko, Swaroop Mishra, Tal Linzen, Tal Schuster, Tao Li, Tao Yu, Tariq Ali, Tatsu Hashimoto, Te-Lin Wu, Théo Desbordes, Theodore Rothschild, Thomas Phan, Tianle Wang, Tiberius Nkinyili, Timo Schick, Timofei Kornev, Titus Tunduny, Tobias Gerstenberg, Trenton Chang, Trishala Neeraj, Tushar Khot, Tyler Shultz, Uri Shaham, Vedant Misra, Vera Demberg, Victoria Nyamai, Vikas Raunak, Vinay Ramasesh, Vinay Uday Prabhu, Vishakh Padmakumar, Vivek Srikumar, William Fedus, William Saunders, William Zhang, Wout Vossen, Xiang Ren, Xiaoyu Tong, Xinran Zhao, Xinyi Wu, Xudong Shen, Yadollah Yaghoobzadeh, Yair Lakretz, Yangqiu Song, Yasaman Bahri, Yejin Choi, Yichi Yang, Yiding Hao, Yifu Chen, Yonatan Belinkov, Yu Hou, Yufang Hou, Yuntao Bai, Zachary Seid, Zhuoye Zhao, Zijian Wang, Zijie J. Wang, Zirui Wang, and Ziyi Wu. 2023. Beyond the imitation game: Quantifying and extrapolating the capabilities of language models. *Preprint*, arXiv:2206.04615.

Alon Talmor, Jonathan Herzig, Nicholas Lourie, and Jonathan Berant. 2019. CommonsenseQA: A question answering challenge targeting commonsense knowledge. In *Proceedings of the 2019 Conference of the North American Chapter of the Association for Computational Linguistics: Human Language Technologies, Volume 1 (Long and Short Papers)*, pages 4149–4158, Minneapolis, Minnesota. Association for Computational Linguistics.

Erik F. Tjong Kim Sang and Fien De Meulder. 2003. Introduction to the CoNLL-2003 shared task: Language-independent named entity recognition. In *Proceedings of the Seventh Conference on Natural Language Learning at HLT-NAACL 2003*, pages 142–147.

Hugo Touvron, Thibaut Lavril, Gautier Izacard, Xavier Martinet, Marie-Anne Lachaux, Timothée Lacroix, Baptiste Rozière, Naman Goyal, Eric Hambro, Faisal Azhar, Aurelien Rodriguez, Armand Joulin, Edouard Grave, and Guillaume Lample. 2023. Llama: Open and efficient foundation language models. *Preprint*, arXiv:2302.13971.

David Vilares and Carlos Gómez-Rodríguez. 2019. HEAD-QA: A healthcare dataset for complex reasoning. In *Proceedings of the 57th Annual Meeting of the Association for Computational Linguistics*, pages 960–966, Florence, Italy. Association for Computational Linguistics.

Alex Wang, Yada Pruksachatkun, Nikita Nangia, Amanpreet Singh, Julian Michael, Felix Hill, Omer Levy, and Samuel R. Bowman. 2019a. SuperGLUE: A stickier benchmark for general-purpose language understanding systems. *arXiv preprint 1905.00537*.

Alex Wang, Amanpreet Singh, Julian Michael, Felix Hill, Omer Levy, and Samuel R. Bowman. 2019b. GLUE: A multi-task benchmark and analysis platform for natural language understanding. In the Proceedings of ICLR.

William Yang Wang. 2017. " liar, liar pants on fire": A new benchmark dataset for fake news detection. *arXiv preprint arXiv:1705.00648*.

Jason Wei, Maarten Bosma, Vincent Y. Zhao, Kelvin Guu, Adams Wei Yu, Brian Lester, Nan Du, Andrew M. Dai, and Quoc V. Le. 2022. Finetuned language models are zero-shot learners. *Preprint*, arXiv:2109.01652.

Ruijie Xu, Zengzhi Wang, Run-Ze Fan, and Pengfei Liu. 2024. Benchmarking benchmark leakage in large language models. *Preprint*, arXiv:2404.18824.

Yi Yang, Wen-tau Yih, and Christopher Meek. 2015. WikiQA: A challenge dataset for open-domain question answering. In *Proceedings of the 2015 Conference on Empirical Methods in Natural Language Processing*, pages 2013–2018, Lisbon, Portugal. Association for Computational Linguistics.

Yinfei Yang, Yuan Zhang, Chris Tar, and Jason Baldridge. 2019. PAWS-X: A Cross-lingual Adversarial Dataset for Paraphrase Identification. In *Proc. of EMNLP*.

Tao Yu, Rui Zhang, Kai Yang, Michihiro Yasunaga, Dongxu Wang, Zifan Li, James Ma, Irene Li, Qingning Yao, Shanelle Roman, Zilin Zhang, and Dragomir Radev. 2018. Spider: A large-scale human-labeled dataset for complex and cross-domain semantic parsing and text-to-SQL task. In *Proceedings of the 2018 Conference on Empirical Methods in Natural Language Processing*, pages 3911–3921, Brussels, Belgium. Association for Computational Linguistics.

Rowan Zellers, Yonatan Bisk, Roy Schwartz, and Yejin Choi. 2018. Swag: A large-scale adversarial dataset for grounded commonsense inference. In *Proceedings of the 2018 Conference on Empirical Methods in Natural Language Processing (EMNLP)*.

Rowan Zellers, Ari Holtzman, Yonatan Bisk, Ali Farhadi, and Yejin Choi. 2019. Hellaswag: Can a machine really finish your sentence? In *Proceedings of the 57th Annual Meeting of the Association for Computational Linguistics*.

Rui Zhang and Joel Tetreault. 2019. This email could save your life: Introducing the task of email subject line generation. *Preprint*, arXiv:1906.03497.

Xiang Zhang, Junbo Zhao, and Yann LeCun. 2015a. Character-level convolutional networks for text classification. In *Advances in Neural Information Processing Systems*, volume 28. Curran Associates, Inc.

Xiang Zhang, Junbo Jake Zhao, and Yann LeCun. 2015b. Character-level convolutional networks for text classification. In *NIPS*.

Yuan Zhang, Jason Baldridge, and Luheng He. 2019. PAWS: Paraphrase Adversaries from Word Scrambling. In *Proc. of NAACL*.

Author Index

Association for Computational Linguistics
209 N. Eighth Street
Stroudsburg, Pennsylvania 18360

CURRAN ASSOCIATES INC.
proceedings.com

ISBN 979-8-3313-0161-3
9 798331 301613